Second to None

T O

None

**The Relentless Drive
and Impossible Dream
of the Super Bowl Bills**

Second

TO

None

**The Relentless Drive
and Impossible Dream
of the Super Bowl Bills**

JOSEPH VALERIO

TRIUMPH
B O O K S

Library of Congress Cataloging-in-Publication Data
Valerio, Joe, 1949-
   Second to none : the relentless drive and impossible dream of the Super Bowl Bills / Joe Valerio ; foreword by Steve Tasker.
   pages cm
   ISBN 978-1-60078-926-7 (hardback)
   1. Buffalo Bills (Football team)—History. 2. Super Bowl—History. I. Title.
   GV956.B83V35 2014
   796.332'640974797—dc23
                         2014005376

This book is available in quantity at special discounts for your group or organization. For further information, contact:

   Triumph Books LLC
   814 North Franklin Street
   Chicago, Illinois 60610
   (312) 337-0747
   www.triumphbooks.com

Printed in U.S.A.

ISBN: 978-1-60078-926-7

Design by James Slate

Photos courtesy of AP Images unless otherwise indicated

For my DC,

Being next to you…

All those Sundays, all those playing fields,
all those great times in our life…

Has been my greatest joy

"You know what they say about the six degrees of separation? Up here it's about three degrees of separation. Everybody is connected. Everybody knows somebody. Fans and players."

—Dick Zolnowski
Buffalo Bills season-ticket holder since 1969

Contents

Foreword

L ET ME TELL you how I became a Buffalo Bill.

I was on the waiver wire with the Houston Oilers because I had been injured, and league rules say you have to be on the waiver wire for 24 hours. They put me on Thursday night at 5:00 PM, and Friday morning when I came in, Jerry Glanville, the Oilers head coach, said there was a phone call for me and that I had been picked up by Buffalo.

I picked up the phone, and this guy on the phone said, "My name is Bo Shempley of the Buffalo Bills," and then he asked, "Has your agent called you about being picked up by Buffalo?"

I said, no, he hadn't. The fact was I didn't have an agent. And he continued, "We'll call you back in about a half hour because we're going to fly you into Buffalo this afternoon."

This was a real shocker and disturbing because I had invited my parents to Houston for the game that Sunday. To make a long story short, I eventually learned from a teammate that it wasn't anyone from the Buffalo Bills on the phone at all, but the Houston conditioning coach playing a joke on me.

The irony of all this is that when I got home that day, the first message on my answering machine was from Bill Polian, the Bills general manager. And this time it was real.

I couldn't help but smile when he told me the news. The next morning I got on a plane and flew to Buffalo and never looked back. People used to ask me if I was unhappy to be going to a team with a 2–14 record. "Not at all," I would tell them. "I was proud that somebody wanted me to play for them."

What I didn't know back then was how much my life was going to change and all for the better. I had grown up in a small town in Kansas called Smith Center, where I played football, basketball, and ran track in high school and later married my high school sweetheart, a cheerleader. If all this sounds very storybookish, it really was. I made my way to Dodge City Community College and then to Northwestern before the Oilers selected me in the ninth round of the 1985 NFL Draft as the 226th player chosen. I wasn't even in Houston for two years before I got the call from Buffalo. But that turned out to be the best call of my life. And the same can be said for just about every one of us who played for the Buffalo Bills in those golden days.

What Joseph Valerio has done here is bring all of us, players and fans and front office people alike, back to that special time for all of Buffalo. And we really did feel like we were second to none. We were all in it together. Buffalo was much more of a small town than a big city. Fans would travel for hours to come to our games, even if it meant driving through snowstorms or sitting in arctic conditions. Long before the Seattle Seahawks celebrated their 12th Man, we knew we had ours everywhere we looked around Ralph Wilson Stadium and throughout the greater Buffalo area.

You'll meet so many of them here, the fans who are the backbone of sports. Fans who would never miss a game and traveled to our Super Bowls. Fans who couldn't wait for training camp to open or for next Sunday to come. Fans who took such pride in our performance and made us feel like part of their families.

Red, white, and Bills blue were the colors of upstate New York. You'd stop at a traffic light, and the fellow in the car next to you would roll down his window to tell you we're going to win this Sunday. It was like that week after week, year after year, for an amazingly long time as we went to four straight Super Bowls—something that had never been done before and has not been done since.

We were able to do this not just because we had great players but because we had great people. The bonds we forged off the field carried us forward on the field. So many of us lived together in Buffalo during the offseason, and so many of us still do, long after our careers have ended because the people of Buffalo have made this a special place through their hard work and dedication, and they still embrace those small town values that I grew up with.

There was a lot more to those Buffalo Bills than those gamedays. And it's all here in this book you are holding. Step back in time with us, as we begin our relentless drive to the Super Bowl.

—Steve Tasker

Introduction

N THIS BOOK, *Second to None*, Joe Valerio has done a magnificent job in capturing the focus, the character, and the unique qualities of those sterling Buffalo Bills teams of the early 1990s. He has also reawakened for me—and he will for all those great football fans in Buffalo and elsewhere also—many fond memories and many emotions that we all experienced during our never-give-up quest for that "impossible dream." He has also conveyed, in real life, examples for everyone who reads this book, a mantra that I always presented to that remarkable group of men whom I am so proud and grateful to have coached, and that mantra is: "Football doesn't *build* character. It *reveals* character."

While almost every good football fan is undoubtedly aware that those Buffalo Bills of the early 1990s were the only team in the history of the National Football League to play in four consecutive Super Bowls, this is a story about much more than just wins and losses. Yes, getting to the Super Bowl was exhilarating. And then losing those games was emotionally crushing.

But what did all the members of our team and organization do after experiencing those heartbreaking losses? Did they just lie there and whimper? Did they give up? Did they throw in the towel? Never! With an almost unparalleled resolve, back at it they went. The road back wasn't an easy one to travel, and Joe Valerio does a wonderful job of providing insights into the character of the people who rose to the challenge. And on that journey, with rare exception, those great Buffalo Bills fans played a role in providing unwavering support for our team. I can, however, recall one minor exception.

That exception came on the Monday after our second loss, when a listener to a call-in show on which I was appearing called in and pleaded, "Coach, please don't go back to next year's Super Bowl game. I can't stand the agony I have felt after we lost these two games. I can't even muster what it takes to go back to work the next day. Please don't go back."

My response was, "Sir, I understand your anguish. I share it. But—I'm glad you're not on my team."

And so, once again, back to work we went. And along the way on that renewed quest, the Buffalo Bills, a wild-card playoff team that year, had to, in the first round of the playoffs, fight their way back from a 35–3, third-quarter deficit in order to win the game. It was the greatest comeback victory in the history of the NFL. After that we still had to win two more road playoff games in order to make it back to Super Bowl Sunday. Somebody said that it couldn't be done, but we did it!

And so, what could be a more perfect title for a book than the one that Joe Valerio has embraced in order to bring us this entire story about a group of players who, in my mind, truly were *Second to None.*

—Marv Levy

CHAPTER 1 | Coalescing in Jim Kelly's Man Cave

EEP INTO THE night, they kept streaming into Jim Kelly's house on Hillsboro Drive, out in the woods of Orchard Park, a short drive from Rich Stadium where, just hours before Kelly and his teammates had demolished the Los Angeles Raiders 51–3 to win the AFC championship and earned a trip to the Super Bowl the following Sunday.

On this January evening in 1991, it seemed like an endless parade of revelries. Among the merrymakers were not just Kelly's teammates, but their families and friends and friends of friends, who had witnessed perhaps the crowning moment in the history of this dignified franchise that had brought so much pride to upstate New York since it entered the old American Football League more than 30 years before. *We're going to the Super Bowl. We're going to the* Super Bowl, Kelly kept thinking to himself as he watched everyone arrive. "I had fulfilled it. It was a dream I'd had ever since I was a little boy," he later said.

It was a dream so many people have, not just NFL players but perhaps millions of kids, of playing quarterback and making the big plays and getting to the big game. Only for Kelly and those gifted few men who ever reach such lofty aspirations to play quarterback in the National Football League, this was no longer a dream, or a goal. It had become a reality.

The feeling was better than he had ever imagined. So many of the people who had meant so much to him over the years were here with him. It almost didn't seem real. "That was the goal all five of my brothers had: to become NFL players," Kelly said. "Fortunately I was able to do it. I was more excited for my brothers, my family, and the city of Buffalo than I really was for myself. I wanted to win it for everybody."

That night, his house was nearly as raucous as the stadium had been that afternoon. Maybe not as loud, but certainly just as boisterous. All the big players in Buffalo, which is to say all of the Bills, were there now and having the time of their lives. They had just won the biggest game any of them had ever played, and they had won big. If possible, they were even more proud than the 80,000 fans who had filled Rich Stadium—no small thing, for the Bills, *their* Bills, meant the world to the people of Buffalo.

"Everybody, the whole team was there," Darryl Talley, the Bills' outstanding linebacker, remembered. "Everybody showed up. Like Robin Hood and his merry little band of men. Everybody was really estatic. We were going to the Super Bowl."

Jim Ritcher, the offensive guard who always made it a point to drop by Kelly's with his family and friends on Sunday nights, said, "It just brought the team closer together. Everyone would just stop by his house. The night wasn't complete unless you were there."

Steve Tasker, the special teams star, knew it was the perfect way to end gameday. "Jim would say, 'You gotta come over,' and I'd say, 'I'd like to, but Mom and Dad are in town, and my brother's around, and I have to do something with them.' And Jim would say, 'Just bring 'em. Bring 'em all over. What fan would not want to come? So it got to the point where everybody's families—Mom, Dad, kids, brothers, sisters—would all be over there. It became more than just players. And you'd see them all there."

If nights like this helped bring them together, well, it had been a long time coming. There had been so many dismal seasons before they became champions. Long, endless years when the Bills went 2–14 back-to-back and then 4–12. Lingering, punishing autumns, often played out in harsh conditions, as the Bills became the joke of the entire league.

Knock, knock.
Who's there?
Owen.
Owen who?
Oh and 10.

For Talley, one of the few veterans who had endured so much pain, it only made this moment all the more gratifying. "As far as the 2–14s, and the 4–12s," Talley would say years later, "there weren't a lot of guys there for that—except for me and Bruce Smith. Jim Kelly went through one. But one thing we all had in common was you got to work real hard to get what you got. Nothing's handed to you. And once we all figured out we had that one thing in common, we all held each other to a higher standard than what anyone else thought [of us]."

It had all come together on an almost balmy January day in Buffalo. The temperature was 36 degrees and a light rain was falling when the Raiders kicked off, just past 12:30 in the afternoon. The game soon turned into a rout. The Bills' high-octane offense could not be contained much less stopped. With Kelly throwing all over the Raiders, Thurman Thomas running by them, and Bruce

Smith, one of the Bills' Big Three who were headed for the Hall of Fame, wreaking havoc on Los Angeles's offensive game plan, Buffalo simply overpowered its opponent.

And on this day, Talley delivered the hallmark game of his Pro Bowl career. He made numerous tackles and had two interceptions, taking the first pick 27 yards into the Raiders end zone to make it a 21–3 Bills stampede. Game, set, and match.

By halftime the score was 41–3. Later, as the clock was winding down, Talley and Smith began slapping each other's shoulder pads in celebration and yelling, "Where are we going?" Smith shouted. "To the show," Talley yelled back. "Where are we going?" Smith screamed once more. "To the show," Talley roared. Then, in unison, they kept laughing and saying, "Next week. Next week. Next week." Then they embraced and were on their way.

Don Pitts, a season-ticket holder, remembers buying a souvenir hat in the parking lot before he entered Rich Stadium that day. "I don't know how they had them yet, but I bought a Buffalo Bills AFC Champions hat," he said. "Of course, I wouldn't wear it going in. I didn't want to jinx them or anything. But at halftime I felt pretty good about what was going on so I put it on. Man, that was a game."

The greatest game any Buffalo team had ever played. The party was on. Tampa, here we come.

Nearly everyone who visited Kelly's home that evening had spent the afternoon cheering wildly for their team dressed in red, white, and blue—appropriate colors for this day in America with the country at war in the Persian Gulf. "Everyone had their Bills paraphernalia on," continued Pitts, a sales representative for Altria. "Whatever items came out, everybody had to have it. The newest and the best. The old Zumba pants, striped red, white, and blue. You wanted the latest and the greatest stuff. You wanted to be seen."

All around the stadium fans could be seen waving American flags. In the days leading up the game there had been concern about terrorist threats, that the war would escalate and force the National Football League to postpone the contest. But the game went on, and the West Point Band performed the national anthem, bringing tears to the eyes of Ralph Wilson Jr., the only owner the Bills had ever had and a World War II veteran.

Wilson was not alone in his sense of pride and accomplishment. The entire municipality of Buffalo had never experienced anything like it. There was no Major League Baseball franchise. The pro basketball team, the Buffalo Braves, had long departed for the West Coast. The hockey team, the Buffalo Sabres, could never elicit the passion of football fans, however long-suffering they were. The Bills' championship seasons of 1964–65 came in the old American Football League before the league merged with the more esteemed National Football League. There was no doubt about it, this was the biggest stage any team representing Buffalo had ever reached. And the Super Bowl, only a week away, was no less than the biggest sporting event in the United States.

"I don't think anyone else on that team had been to a Super Bowl," Talley said, "front office or anything. The team was charged up. You played, worked all your life to get to this game, to get to this point, and it was one of the days when [you do] whatever it takes to win. It was a chance to get to the Super Bowl. And everybody thinks about doing it, but now you have the power to get yourself there. Everybody was as happy as they could be. But there was still a one-win game."

Upon arriving at Kelly's house, all the guests, and there were easily a 100 of them now, promptly made their way downstairs to where his state-of-the-art entertainment center, sprawled across the basement of his spacious home, was switched on. The massive television set—"one of those big refrigerator-size things," Steve Tasker recalled—was showing the final seconds of the National Football Conference title game out in San Francisco. The New York Giants were about to upset the two-time Super Bowl–champion 49ers on the final play of the game, a 42-yard field goal by Matt Bahr, his fifth field goal of the day, that would send the Giants on to Tampa with a 15–13 victory.

By then Smith had settled into his customary place, a front-row seat on the huge couch next to Kelly, as they always did on these Sunday nights, so no one could block their view as they watched *SportsCenter* on ESPN and then the VHS tape of their game from that afternoon. For the Bills, this was like watching their own installment of *Masterpiece Theater* over and over again, much to the delight of an adoring crowd of Buffalo insiders.

Ritcher, a lineman, remembers those nights like they were yesterday—how his parents and groups of friends would drive up from Ohio for every game and afterward they would all go to Ilio DiPaolo's, a popular Italian restaurant in Buffalo and then make a final stop at Kelly's house.

Pete Metzelaars, the big tight end, loved going to Ilio's. "Almost 20 guys on the team would go there after the game. He kept the whole back room isolated for us. We came in a back entrance and we'd have dinner. Kind of kick back, relax a little bit, talk about the game a little bit. We all had our families and kids, and that was the place to be after the games."

"My father and the players would come in after the game," Dennis DiPaolo recalled, "and my father would always have his friend tape the game. Then when we came back we'd put the tape in so the players could watch while they were eating with their families. Kent Hull, Will Wolford, Jim Ritcher, Andre Reed—they wanted to hear what Don Criqui was saying about them. They really enjoyed watching a nationally televised game while they were sitting eating dinner. You never got tired of watching the game."

"Then a lot of times, after dinner we'd take the kids home," Metzelaars said, "and get a babysitter and go to Jim Kelly's house." He laughs at the memory of it now: fairly nice neighborhood, big houses and stuff, cars parked up and down the street. That poor neighborhood got invaded every Sunday night when there was a home game."

It had become a ritual, and not only did it bring the team closer together, but it reinforced the bond with some of the Bills' great players from the past who were always welcome. And in Buffalo, and throughout America, no Bill was more famous than O.J. Simpson, the celebrated Heisman Trophy winner who had been one of the greatest running backs in NFL history and led Buffalo's last rise to prominence in the early '70s. O.J.'s fame had only increased after his playing days, through television broadcasting, commercials, and movies. "Of course, this was before the O.J. Simpson incident," Ritcher said. "O.J. would be on one of Jim's couches watching the replay of our game with Thurman [Thomas] with my friends from Ohio sitting between them. And one of them looked over at me, like she couldn't believe it, and she'd say, 'O.J. can you pass the chips?' Stuff like that was just so incredible for someone like that from Ohio."

The real centerpiece of Kelly's man cave was a long bar accented by a huge mirror bearing the inscription KELLY'S IRISH PUB. At one end of the bar was a dance floor and at the other end was the huge, rear-projection TV. In still another corner of the room sat a large pool table that seldom lacked activity. Don Beebe was a fixture there, shooting pool even on a Sunday night like this, with the broken leg he had suffered a month earlier in a game against the Miami Dolphins. The downstairs doors fanned out to a huge backyard that contained a bocce court.

Situated on a quiet cul-de-sac with only a handful of neighbors, the surroundings could not have been more beneficial to Kelly. A bachelor, he had the spacious, 7,500-square-foot custom home built not long after he arrived in Buffalo in 1986 with the then-most-lucrative contract in the game. This was a place where his parents and five brothers would be able to stay when they came to visit, which was often, since the Kellys were a close-knit group. And the home afforded every luxury of a five-star hotel, which were in short supply in Buffalo. It featured eight bedrooms, six bathrooms, a sauna, a steam room, two Jacuzzis, and of course, a magnificent finished basement.

It served his needs well since it afforded privacy, a currency in short supply for the celebrated quarterback of an adored team in this small city in upstate New York. After all, his was the face of the Buffalo Bills, and at 6′3″ and 225 pounds, he clearly stood out in a crowd. And in a municipality as small as Buffalo that notoriety can be suffocating as well as intoxicating. It surely made it difficult to go out and socialize without drawing attention.

He was young and handsome and single, the trifecta, to say nothing of his wealth. If fans thought he had the perfect life, they often expected—damn well demanded—perfection from him on the field, and nothing less than civility in public.

There had been times in the past when Kelly would be out on the town and fans would shower him with much more than affection. On one particular evening there had been an incident with a woman in a nightclub. "Jim said something she didn't appreciate," Bob Koshinski, a local television reporter for WKBW-TV remembered, "and she threw a drink at him and I think he put her up against the wall according to stories. And our station, we were the number-one news station in town, and, of course, we had a reporter out at his house in the early-morning hours. And his dad came to the door and sent her away and Jim refused to talk to us for a week or two, till he got over it."

A few years after the incident, Bills management was only too happy when Kelly began inviting his teammates back to his home after games, far from public view, to kick back and let the good times roll. "Not that we didn't have a good relationship with the fans," Ritcher said, "but there was always a chance guys would go out and get in trouble when we were starting to be fairly successful. Being an offensive lineman, you're never that noticeable. And I wasn't a big name up there, but everyone would seem to recognize you and ask, 'Hey, how're you doing?' It was nice. It was always great to be a Buffalo Bill."

Mark Kelso, a safety, who by his own admission "wasn't a well-known guy" remembered how he couldn't go anywhere without attracting attention. "Driving around, they'd wave or say hi to you in a very respectful way. Of course, they'd want autographs every once in a while, but they were only too happy to be part of us, and proud of us, and winning only accentuated it more. We were part of the fabric of western New York. There's no question."

By the time Kelso finally made it home later that night to pack for the Super Bowl, his neighbors had draped a big sign over his house: TAMPA HERE WE COME. "I think they felt every bit of the excitement we felt as players," he said.

Throughout the downstairs room at Kelly's home, there were platters of food, heaping portions of burgers, slabs of beef, and chicken and chicken wings, Buffalo-style—a local favorite that would soon sweep the nation. There were also a few bartenders who kept opening cases of beer, wine, vodka, and, on this night to remember, even several cases of Dom Perignon champagne. "The best of the best," Cornelius Bennett remembered. "Jim always took care of us." On this special night, with the Super Bowl in sight, Bennett remembered a distinctive touch: "Each bottle of champagne was engraved with the player's name."

There was never trouble keeping the good times flowing at Kelly's Irish Pub, but then they had never celebrated an occasion quite like this.

Dennis DiPaolo, whose father ran the popular restaurant in town, remembers catering Kelly's parties. "One of the keys to the Bills' success was that Jim was a leader and he did a lot of team functions with everybody," DiPaolo said. "All those parties at his house after games, they were something. They used to call them 'the bickering Bills.' Maybe you saw that on the field, but after the game they were all having dinner together with their families, high-fiving, laughing. They were one big family."

For a time they had been a dysfunctional family. All that may have been in the past now. But more than a few of these Bills could not help but think how far they had all come to realize this shining moment. Midway through the '89 season, Kelly suffered a separated shoulder, a critical blow for a quarterback who had a big arm and loved to throw deep. It happened in Indianapolis, when Colts defender Jon Hand came in virtually untouched and leveled Kelly. It hardly mattered that Kelly managed to complete that pass, a 16-yard touchdown to Andre Reed; the Bills were far behind by then in a game they would lose 37–14. What really mattered was the way Kelly handled himself after the game when he lashed out at his offensive line and the young African American tackle Howard Ballard in particular. Kelly felt Ballard was the "weak link" who enabled Hand to crush his shoulder into the Astroturf.

The following day, with his shoulder tightly wrapped, Kelly didn't back off his comments. The next day, Thomas, the star running back and an African American, took a shot at his quarterback. The media in Buffalo soon christened their team "the bickering Bills." Nice. It was to became the stuff of legends.

It hardly mattered when Kelly rescinded his comments later that week because the damage had been done. The dirty laundry had been hung out in full public view, and the stain would remain in the locker room for some time. "After Jim made that comment about Howard Ballard, Buffalonians will recall that forced news conference when Marv Levy made Jim Kelly and Thurman Thomas stand side-by-side at the podium and basically agree to get along," Koshinski said. "Jim suffered a shoulder injury and basically pointed the finger at Ballard. Thurman took it upon himself to come out on the media day, Wednesday, to point a finger at Kelly and say that they could use help at the quarterback position. That got everybody fired up, and Marv really made the two of them come in and read a written statement. All of us in the media knew the whole thing was a sham."

Years later, Kelly would wince when the subject was broached. He would cite his lack of maturity and acknowledge that there are things better left unsaid before the media. And he expressed gratitude that he was not playing in today's world of 24/7 news coverage. When pressed, Kelly would respond tersely, "Let's move on to the next question."

"Jim didn't handle the media all that well," Tasker recalled. "He didn't lead from the head but from the mouth. The media was just starting to become what it is today. Jim was the only quarterback in the league who would have press conferences to explain what he said the day before, to backtrack. "But the thing about it, and it overrode everything, is that no matter what, that freakin' guy never forgot his friends or his teammates. His heart was in the right place. He would have lit himself on fire to win a game. And the guys appreciated it and would do anything for him because of that. He wouldn't take a play off. He'd throw an interception and run the guy down trying to make a tackle. That bought a lot back from those guys in the locker room."

If nothing else, the Bills were a fiery group. In the second week of this Super Bowl season, the Bills were badly beaten in Miami, 30–7. With a little more than eight minutes remaining in the game, Levy conceded defeat and pulled some of his stars out of the game. "It was tee-off time on the quarterback, so I took Kelly out," Levy said. "Our chances of winning were small so we wanted to save our front liners from the possibility of injury."

One of those men on the front lines, Bruce Smith, bristled at being removed from the game. He got into a heated argument on the sideline with the coach and complained that Levy had given up. The coach responded by fining his star defensive end $500.

Levy also fined Leonard Smith, Nate Odomes, and Kirby Jackson $100 each—insubordination for not leaving the field promptly.

Levy wasn't about to go through another locker room insurrection like he had the year before with Kelly and Ballard. He was determined to blunt the conflict and said, "To say I just ignored what happened last year would be foolhardy." Levy was fully aware that the moniker "the bickering Bills" had caught on. "It has a nice ring to it," he admitted drily to reporters.

What Levy did next may have saved Buffalo's season. He arranged for a group of team leaders to examine the team's complaints and act as a liaison with the coaching staff. It was a master stroke. The players were now held accountable. They came together as never before and would finish their work week on Sunday nights at Kelly's.

It all came back to the quarterback, as it almost always does in football. The quarterback is the centerpiece of the game and the team. All action flows from him. Accordingly, Kelly had signed the most lucrative contract in football when he came to Buffalo from the suddenly defunct United States Football League in 1986, signing an eye-popping five-year package worth $8 million. He was their star quarterback, their franchise player, the man with the golden arm who was hired to lift the Bills to the top of the football world. All that money commanded attention. Still, it took time to truly exude leadership.

Perhaps it could be said the Bills' ascent began during the 1988 season, when Kelly started inviting some teammates back to his house after their home games. Those Sunday nights, and a lot of wins on Sunday afternoons, sure went a long way toward fostering goodwill. "All those Sunday nights," Kelly said, "all those parties and having all my teammates there, that was the start of something very, very special, bringing everybody to my house after football games. And to have everybody celebrate with their families, with everybody else, not just the players with each other but have families meet each other, wives meet each other, girlfriends meet each other, that is what is important. That is why we always thought we had one of the closest teams you could possibly get in the NFL. That's what we realized early on. That's what made us so strong. That's what made us so close."

"No doubt that helped form bonds and break down barriers," recalled linebacker Ray Bentley. "That's what I give Kelly the most credit for: how open he was with his home and how important it was to him to get everybody in that kind of environment."

Bonds.

Solidarity.

And so they became united in one common cause: winning.

Finally, after so many difficult losing campaigns, they were the newly christened champions of the AFC. The Bills had finally arrived. Their signature identity was the no-huddle, hurry-up offense, which made it difficult for defenses to align their schemes, much less substitute their players, as the Bills rapidly ran off one play after another.

Ange Coniglio has lived in Buffalo all his life and has been going to Bills games from their very beginning. He was an engineer for the Army Corps of Engineers and also taught engineering at the University of Buffalo. He was drawn to the precision of the no-huddle offense, how it changed the game and the way it disrupted the Raiders in the AFC Championship Game. "I liked to talk to the players about the greatness of the no-huddle offense when we crossed paths," he said. "The flashiness of it, and how it would make other teams stop and take their breath. One of my fondest memories is that 51–3 rout of the Raiders, when the Raiders took a timeout in the first drive of the first period as the Bills drove down the field because they didn't know what to do or how to stop 'em. And that was fantastic."

From their opening drive that day, when Kelly bobbled a snap from his center in the shotgun formation, and the ball bounded up into his hands and he managed to find James Lofton with a 13-yard touchdown pass, everything went Buffalo's way. When Thomas darted into the end zone from 12 yards out to end the Bills' second possession, the score was 14–3 and the Raiders were reeling.

Not long thereafter, Jay Schroeder, the Raiders' quarterback, was pressured by Bruce Smith and his errant pass landed right in the hands of Talley, who carried it into the end zone and set off a frenzied celebration throughout Rich Stadium. Right then and there, Talley could have pretty much picked up the Lamar Hunt Trophy that goes to the champion of the AFC, but formality dictated that a full 60 minutes had to be played in any event.

Afterward, when a reporter asked Kelly to describe a particular scoring play, the quarterback looked confused and, for once, at a loss for words. "Gee, there were so many," he said. "I can't remember that one."

But years later he could still remember the feeling that came over him that day. "I just remember everything clicking from the time I fumbled the snap and went to pick it up and my helmet snapped up in my face and I scrambled and threw one to James Lofton that he caught, and it went for a touchdown."

It had been that day and now it was this kind of night to celebrate. "Kelly's house was the highlight of the week," center Kent

Hull said. "Especially on days when we knew we couldn't be beat. We couldn't wait to get to his house. It was like Bourbon Street."

The Bills had a special bond, a true brotherhood, Talley believed. "In the offseason we played basketball with each other. A lot of guys would hunt with each other. We'd go to movies, go bowling together. Whenever anybody wanted to do something, all he had to do was tell one or two guys and then you got 25 or 30 guys and here we go."

"We knew so much more about each other than other teams did," Tasker recalled. "Nobody lived more than 20 minutes apart. You'd go to San Diego or New York, guys would never see each other away from the building. Because we were way up in Buffalo, we had nobody else to party with or go to dinner with. So there weren't these extracurricular entourages. We were like a big family. It didn't matter whether you were with your mom and dad, or my mom and dad, and that just really enlarged the chemistry on that team. It was unmatched. It became bigger than just the players on the field. People knew who we were and we were hard not to like. We loved each other, and it was great. I think that's one of the cool things about that team."

So many of the Bills lived in Orchard Park, close enough to make the drive home after a big night at Jim's without incident. And for those who weren't up to driving, well, Jim always seemed to have one of his guys, like Dave Irwin, around to lend a helping hand. Irwin ran a limousine company and he could always be counted on to make the final rounds of the night around Buffalo. And those who had simply partied too hearty were free to crash at Kelly's.

It was a Sunday night that seemed like so many others, until you turned back the clock on the day's events. And no one appreciated this more than Kelly. "I grew up in Pittsburgh watching the Steelers go to all those Super Bowls," the quarterback fairly beamed. "And now I'm going to my first Super Bowl. And our goal is to win it. Twenty years down the road, I don't want people to say the Bills were in it, but they didn't win it. Our goal is to win it."

Kelly and his teammates were living the life. They were young and successful and at the top of their game. And they knew it and appreciated it and reveled in it. Throughout the night they raised their glasses and made toasts saluting their good fortune and their dream yet to come. In a few hours, just after dawn, they would all be packed and ready to fly to Tampa. United as never before to play one more game, this time for the championship of all football.

There was only one thing mattered.

Only one thing they wanted: a Super Bowl ring.

They had no way of knowing how hard it would be to get one.

CHAPTER 2 | **Bill Polian's Building Blocks**

A s THE BILLS touched down in Tampa for Super Bowl week, their general manager, Bill Polian, couldn't help but remember those bleak days years before when he first arrived in Buffalo, and Rich Stadium wasn't even half-filled on Sunday afternoons. One of the first issues he confronted was how to lure fans back to the stadium on gameday. It didn't take him long to develop a marketing plan that made the games more affordable for the blue-collar citizens of western New York. Under Polian's direction season tickets became available at a discounted package price from those sold on a game-by-game basis. Furthermore, he had the Bills play only one preseason game—not two—at home, effectively cutting the cost of those worthless exhibitions in half.

Soon his innovations began to pay off, and fans began to return to one of the coldest venues in professional sports. After all the losing seasons, these were still their Buffalo Bills and fans felt an uncommon sense of attachment to them. "We'd always see the Bills, come in contact with them," said one of their longtime fans, Dick Zolnowski, who had followed the team since their first days at War Memorial Stadium. "At the old stadium, we were practically right down there on the field. And after the games, the players would come out of their dressing rooms and they'd be right there on the street. You could walk right up and talk to them. It was a different time."

Then the new stadium went up, bringing a surge of pride throughout the city. "We stood out there all the time watching it go up," Zolnowski remembered. "We were one of the first ones to have a Jumbotron. The image wasn't as sharp as what we have now. It was almost like cartoon-type characters rather than regular TV-type pictures. Years later we went to another screen and then a third screen. But in those days, it was something new."

And in those days, the fans would thrill to replays on the Jumbotron of O.J. Simpson running like a wild buffalo, setting rushing records, gaining a record 2,003 yards in the 14-game 1973 season. The Juice was as big a star as there was in the game, a huge national celebrity, but in Buffalo he had an almost small-town aura about him. He was that rarest of supernovas: a downright accessible superstar. "Back in the '70s, that's when we had our first big mall, Eastern Hills Mall, and on Mondays, the players' day off back then, you'd run into O.J. Simpson there," Zolnowski said. "And he always stopped and signed autographs. You'd run into him there just about every Monday."

When Polian took the reins of the Bills, he believed the fans yearned for a team they could identify with, a team they could embrace and believe in. From an early age, Polian had understood what a team could mean to a community, how it could lift the spirit of an entire city. And he learned this as a young boy, who was nurtured by two of the most revered franchises of his time. Back when his father's family came to America and settled in Brooklyn, it was all but considered a sacrament to root for the Dodgers and pay your respects at Ebbets Field. But as a youngster,

Polian's family moved to the Bronx, and he became a frequent visitor to Yankee Stadium, accompanied by his grandfather, who was a passionate fan of the Yankees. And so Polian came to appreciate the two perennial winners who defined their boroughs, though his heart belonged to the Yankees, the most dominant team in American sports. Still, when the Dodgers departed for the West Coast, Polian clearly understood the heartbreak that enveloped Brooklyn, a heartache that never healed.

Following the Bills' consecutive 2–14 seasons in the early '80s, the worst stretch in their history and one of the most dismal of any team's in pro football, Polian sensed that the future of the Buffalo franchise was precarious at best. Attendance was dwindling, and the Bills had become such an embarrassment that bumper stickers entreating BRING FOOTBALL BACK TO BUFFALO had become as prevalent as presidential campaign stickers. There was widespread concern that the Bills would leave Buffalo and abandon all of western New York. As Polian often remarked, his promotion came on December 30, 1985, "When hopes were low, and snow was high."

"I think the perception was always more difficult than the reality," Polian would say about those tenuous times in Buffalo when there was much talk of the Bills relocating—persistent rumors that owner Ralph Wilson had to repeatedly deflect. "Mr. Wilson has said many times that he never contemplated moving the Bills," Polian said. "However, in 1984 when I got there and then following the two, 2–14 seasons that took place over that time, the team became sort of the butt of Johnny Carson jokes. And, as in the case in politics, when you become the punch line on a late-night television show, the perception is never good."

Polian didn't kid himself about how serious the plight of the Bills—and Buffalo—really was. "There was a confluence of bad luck. The loss of 77,000 jobs and 270,000 people when the steel industry collapsed and the blizzards of '77 and '85, which paralyzed the region. In my first season there, we went 2–14, and I think we had about 35,000 in the stadium for our game with Cleveland at the end of the season on an awful day when it was sleeting and snowing. Then the day they announced that I was the general manager, the first person I saw was the ticket manager, who said, 'Congratulations. You should know that we have sold only 12,000 season tickets right now.' Capacity was 77,000 at the time. Maybe the team wasn't in danger of leaving, but obviously everywhere the perception wasn't good."

If the good people of Buffalo had failed to set the bar very high for Polian, well that was their problem, not his. He was determined. And driven. And confident.

But he was hardly a high-profile choice the year before when he joined the Bills as the new director of pro personnel. Upon his first encounter with Larry Felser, *The Buffalo News'* highly regarded sportswriter, in a hotel lobby, Polian half-jokingly introduced himself, by saying, "I'm Bill Who." In the parlance of the day, he told it like it was. "We were 2–14 on merit," Polian said on the day he became the GM. "We have the worst personnel in the NFL." But he also displayed the confidence that would help transform the Bills: "I know the NFL well. I know its players. I think I'm prepared for the job."

He was plainspoken, not brash, and he was smart. As a young scout with the Kansas City Chiefs, he developed a sharp eye for talent. Soon after he arrived in Buffalo, he gained on-the-job experience when Bills general manager Terry Bledsoe suffered a heart attack. It fell to Polian, along with the director of scouting Norm Pollom, to handle contract negotiations until Bledsoe recovered, and one of his first responsibilites was to sign Bruce Smith, the very first pick in the draft out of Virginia Tech. Polian signed him, and the first of the Bills Super Bowl pieces was in place. Not long thereafter, Bledsoe was fired, and Polian was promoted. Smith and Jim Kelly would mark the turning points in the Bills ascent. "The draft of '85," Polian said fondly, "we went into that draft convinced that we had to hit a home run. Of course, we had the first pick and we had to do all that we could to infuse young talent because the Bills had gotten older." Along with Smith, Polian selected Andre Reed and Frank Reich, who would both play vital roles in Buffalo's future success.

His next task would turn out to be the most important in Buffalo's history, and Polian was more than up to the job. He had to lure Kelly from the floundering United State Football League and convince him to come to Buffalo. Everyone in Buffalo had heard what Kelly moaned as he watched on television when the Bills drafted him two years earlier: "Why did *they* have to take me?"

It wasn't a secret in 1983 that Kelly had never wanted to be in Buffalo. And it certainly wasn't a secret three years later, in 1986, as the USFL was collapsing. "No way did he want to come to Buffalo," recalled Bob Koshinski, a reporter for ABC affiliate WKBW-TV who broke the story that Kelly had signed with the Bills. "When he was in the USFL, the Bills weren't very good. And I remember monitoring satellite interviews that he had done, where he said he wanted to go play originally for the Pittsburgh Steelers because he was a Pittsburgh boy and he also wanted to go play for the Raiders because he liked the swagger of Al Davis. I remember being in a satellite interview room one day, and he was trying to put together a contract—the Bills had the right to match anybody's offer. And [Davis] was going to put a building into his contract, either a building located in Pittsburgh or a building located in Oakland and he figured no way Buffalo could match a real estate offer."

Kelly was near tears when the Bills picked him in the illustrious NFL draft of 1983 that harvested one of the richest crop of quarterbacks the game has ever known.

John Elway was the first quarterback taken followed by Todd Blackledge. Then Kelly began to wait out the first round, hoping one of the teams he had rooted for as a boy in Pennsylvania, the Steelers or the Raiders, would draft him. It was a long shot at best; other talented young passers including Tony Eason, Ken O'Brien, and Dan Marino were all waiting to be selected. "I remember hearing that Elway didn't want to play for the Baltimore Colts," Kelly told ESPN in a *30 for 30* documentary about the 1983 draft. "So a couple of picks later my agent turns to me and says, 'Jim, is there anyone you don't want to play for?'

"Oh, yeah. I went to the University of Miami. *Florida,*" Kelly quickly replied with special emphasis on the Sunshine State. Then the young quarterback rattled off his death list. "I don't want to play for the Minnesota Vikings. I don't want to play for the Green Bay Packers. And I sure don't want to play for the Buffalo Bills."

Kelly was watching the draft with his parents, nervously waiting for his name to be called. The Bills, holding two spots in the first round, finally had their first selection, the 12th pick. "I'm sitting there with my parents. My mother was on the left arm of the chair, and my dad was on the right arm of the chair, and suddenly it's the 12th pick of the first round of the draft, and I'm sitting there saying, 'Please don't pick me. Please don't pick me.'"

As Kelly held his breath, NFL commissioner Pete Rozelle stepped to the lectern and said, "With the 12th pick of the draft the Buffalo Bills select tight end Tony Hunter of Notre Dame."

In his parents' living room, Kelly jumped out of his seat and signalled touchdown with his arms raised. "I knocked my mother on the ground," he immediately realized. "'I'm sorry, Mom.' Then I pick my mother up. I'm not going to Buffalo."

Right before the next pick, Kelly's agent reminded him the Bills also had the 14th pick in the first round. It turned out that Buffalo's vice president of player personel, Norm Pollom, had planned on going for Tony Hunter with his first pick because he believed Kelly and Marino would still be available, "and we were going to get one of them."

After the Detroit Lions chose James Jones, a running back from Florida, Rozelle returned to the microphone, and, as was his custom, intoned with dramatic pauses: "With the 14th pick… Buffalo selects…quarterback Jim Kelly…Miami of Florida."

Kelly was distraught but soon composed himself in a telephone interview with Bob Ley during ESPN's draft coverage. Ley wanted to know if Kelly was surprised to be selected by Buffalo. "No, from the beginning I sorta thought it was going to be Buffalo," Kelly feigned. "I read articles. I talked to so many people. I want to thank the Buffalo Bills for having the interest in picking me and I'm grateful to be part of the Buffalo Bills organization."

Nothing could have been further from the truth. Years later Kelly would shake his head, crack a smile, and say, "You have to say those things. It's just part of selling yourself to the franchise that picked you, of course. Those are lies."

By the time the Miami Dolphins had used the next-to-last pick in the first round to draft Dan Marino, Kelly was already contemplating his options. They were basically the United States Football League, which played ball in the spring and for which he had been drafted by the Chicago Blitz, or the Canadian Football League, where it is even colder and more remote than Buffalo. No matter what Kelly decided, the Bills would retain his rights to play in the NFL for four years, whether or not he came to terms with them. Neither Pittsburgh nor Oakland would be an option.

Privately, Kelly told his agents to make the best deal they could away from Buffalo. Publicly, he went through the motions of visiting Buffalo shortly after the draft only to discover that the Bills' other top picks, Hunter and Darryl Talley, were hardly enthusiastic about beginning their professional careers with such a downtrodden team. When the three draft picks were introduced at the Buffalo Quarterback Club luncheon, all of them had a hard time putting on a happy face. However, the Bills' veteran players were most welcoming when the rookies arrived to take part in mini-camp, knowing how much help the team needed to rebuild.

By then Kelly was pretty much resigned to the idea that he was going to play for the Buffalo Bills—so much so that he was about to sign a contract when a secretary interrupted the meeting to say there was a very important phone call that Kelly had to take.

Bruce Allen, the general manager of the Chicago Blitz of the USFL, was on the line. "For some reason they put me through," Allen said. "Kelly's agent told me the Bills don't even know who I'm talking to. I said, 'Well, don't tell them who you're talking to. You gotta get out of those offices. We'll talk tonight. There's no way they won't pay you more if you walk out of there, and I promise you the USFL will pay you more than that."

When Kelly left the room without signing, the Bills' executives were devastated. "When he walked out I knew we had lost him," said Norm Pollom.

The USFL, desperate for stars, and especially star quarterbacks, basically asked Kelly to pick the field of his dreams. His agents were able to negotiate a sweetheart deal on the eve of the league's second season. "They said, 'Who do you want to play for? We just need to get top quarterbacks into this league,'" Kelly recalled. "I remember going to Houston—the Houston Gamblers. Playing in a domed stadium, no wind, no rain—pretty much a quarterback's dream. That talked me into it."

The new league was risky business, but they were talking silly money, and it didn't take Kelly long to figure out which way the wind was blowing. "Would you rather be in Houston or Buffalo? Stop there," he said.

So what if the new league played in the spring, and football fans weren't flocking to their TV sets, let alone its stadiums? The Gamblers were willing to throw out millions to attract Kelly: $3.5 million over five years, with the first million guaranteed, even if they never fielded a team.

And so Kelly found his way deep into the heart of Texas and the pockets of Jerry Argovitz, whose new expansion team, the Gamblers, would be playing in the air-conditioned Houston Astrodome, "the eighth wonder of the world." It was about as far away from the bleak wintry conditions prevalent in Buffalo as Kelly was likely to get.

It was mad money in those days. The Gamblers were betting that Kelly would provide a star persona like Joe Namath had for the fledgling American Football League a generation before. Ralph Wilson, as a charter owner of the AFL, always remembered how Namath's famous $427,000 contract—an outrageous sum in the mid-'60s—more than solidified the league. It gave the AFL credibility and changed the face not just of professional football but of professional sports. With Kelly gone to the USFL, Wilson did the only thing he could: he held on to Kelly's rights and prayed that the newfangled USFL would go under. The sooner, the better.

As it turned out, despite signing several stars such as Herschel Walker, who won the Heisman trophy, and charismatic quarterbacks including Doug Flutie and Steve Young, the USFL folded two years later when it failed to win a $1.69 billion antitrust lawsuit against the NFL. That $1 million signing bonus Kelly was to receive? Well, to this day he's still owed some $300,000 of it, but his time in Texas nevertheless paid off. Kelly put in a couple of years under the dome, threw a ton of passes, won a bunch of games, and none of it did anything to hurt his stock. He was a hot commodity.

When Wilson's prayers were finally answered, Kelly had little recourse but to head back to Buffalo or keep going even farther, north of the border to Canada. His next move was preordained to become a union born of practicality and necessity: Buffalo, New York. "If I were to trade Jim Kelly's rights, this team would no longer be in Buffalo," Wilson wasn't afraid to tell the quarterback's agents. "We would get booed right out of town."

And so it was in the early afternoon of August 18, 1986, as Ralph Wilson's private jet pulled into Greater Buffalo International Airport, that Kelly could hardly believe the sight outside his window. Television camera crews and newspaper photographers vied for the best vantage point on the tarmac to document the arrival of the 26-year-old quarterback who had just come to contractual terms with the Buffalo Bills.

Their Buffalo Bills.

A local TV reporter handed Kelly a football and urged him to make his first pass as a Bill, and Kelly cooperated, tossing a softball that was easy to handle—just what the cameras wanted. Then Kelly posed with the Bills owner, holding up his newly minted jersey, bearing the number 12. Having completed that photo op, they entered the back seat of a black Lincoln limousine that was parked nearby and headed onto the freeway for the drive downtown and a press conference that had been years in the making. As soon as they reached the highway, Kelly began taking in more scenes that defied his imagination. Hundreds of fans, maybe even thousands, were stationed along the sides of the Kensington Freeway and straddling the overpass of the highway, holding signs proclaiming, WE LOVE YOU, JIM and, get this, WELCOME BACK.

It had been a long and circuitous route that had brought Kelly back to Buffalo. His whole football career had been about getting past bumps in the road. But his outlook was always quite simple: you get knocked down, you get back up. And move on. "You throw an interception, *boom*, it's gone. Learn from it," he said. "Do something about it. Don't feel sorry for yourself. What can I do to make this situation better?"

Kelly can take you through all the ups and downs in his career in about as much time as it takes to break from the huddle, recognize the defense, call an audible, and unload a pass. "From the time I went to Penn State football camp in my junior and senior years in high school, I wanted to play football at Penn State. And I thought I was gonna be a Nittany Lion until Joe Paterno said he wanted me as a linebacker," Kelly said. "And going to the University of Miami, and I was all excited, and then [I had] to run the veer offense, which is totally not my style. I'm ready to transfer, and then Howard Schnellenberger comes in, and then I work my way up to backup quarterback. And then my first start ever as a college quarterback was as a redshirt freshman at Penn State, and we upset them. My first four starts as a college quarterback were Penn State, Alabama, Notre Dame, and Florida. Unreal. A 19-year-old kid from Pennsylvania. And then my senior year, I'm touted for the Heisman Trophy, I blow my right shoulder out, and they insert three metal rods in it and tell me I'll never play football again. And being drafted by the Buffalo Bills and not wanting to play here."

All this was running through Kelly's mind now like some videotape on fast forward, just the way he liked it, like his hurry-up offense, as the limo made its way toward downtown Buffalo. "I wasn't really sure how they were gonna accept me because there were years when I said I would never become a Buffalo Bill," Kelly would recall long after he retired. "It was nothing like what I ever expected."

"They got on what is called 'the 33,' Route 33, a major high-way that goes downtown," one of the Bills oldest and most loyal fans, Donn Bartz, recalled. "By the time they come down to City Hall, where we had this big traffic circle, I don't think you could have moved. Camera crews, television stations, so many people jammed in there and tying up traffic. If you could get off from work you were there. Everybody was excited. Everybody just felt, 'We're going to the Super Bowl.' I don't think most of us felt it was going to happen the next year. We just felt we had a shot now. It just picked us right up, let's put it that way. It was a great feeling."

Over at Rich Stadium, more than 1,000 season tickets were sold that day, and that number would swell to 3,000 by the end of the week. By then Kelly was feeling very much a Buffalo Bill, very much at home. Bill Polian had a lot to do with making his homecoming a relatively smooth transition.

From their first meeting, Kelly and Polian got along well. "I thought we had a very good chance of signing Jim because of the kind of person he was," Polian said years later. "I didn't think his agents were very much in our corner, but I thought Jim would accept and embrace the challenge. And when I had a chance to meet him in New York and I explained to him how the team was constructed, that he could come into a team that was in pretty good shape offensively—with Andre Reed and Ronnie Harmon, receivers like that, Pete Metzelaars, and Jim Ritcher—you know, I think he had a little different view of things. Wow, this is a team that's got a chance. It's not Siberia, as the agents and certain people of the press had pictured it.

"So I made it clear to Jim: you're the last piece of the puzzle, and there will be things we'll do defensively to get better, but in terms for somebody to lead this team, be the face of the franchise, and turn it around, it's you. And that challenge, and that opportunity, doesn't exist anywhere else. And there's nobody better to do it than a tough, hard-nosed guy from western Pennsylvannia playing in front of your family every week. And I expected that would interest him, and challenge him, and it did, obviously."

It was a sales pitch that resonated with Kelly: "Bill Polian was a blue-collar guy. He was like the people I grew up with: blue-collar people in Pennsylvania, where you did your job and worked hard and never took a day off. He wanted people with a strong work ethic to come in here and be a part of this. He wanted strong, self-motivated players. That's what he looked for."

"Bill Polian was about as fiery a general manager as you would find," Koshinski said. "You wouldn't find anybody more loyal to his players than Bill. If you said something about one of his players, he took it personally. I was very good friends with a gentleman, Art Wander, a longtime radio guy who worked in many major markets across the country and who even met the Beatles. He was really a music guy, but he came to Buffalo relatively late in his life and he was doing a little sports talk show, a one-hour show on a weak AM station. And he came on one day after the Bills had lost to New Orleans and said they needed to make a change at offensive coordinator, and it coincided with Larry Felser writing a critical article. Now Polian was at the Monday Quarterback Club luncheon and he did what became his famous get-out-of-town speech."

It was December 11, 1989, and Polian was fuming, as much about what the radio guy said as how his team played. "Jim Kelly's still the quarterback, and Ted Marchibroda's still the offensive coordinator, and Marv Levy's still the head coach," Polian said. "And if you don't like it, get out of town," he said.

"It went down as one of Bill's most famous moments," Kochinski said, and the memory still brings a smile to his face decades later. "It really propelled Art. Everybody wanted to know who this guy was on this little radio station. Art, he ended up getting a real nice gig out of it on this little sports radio station in town."

It turned out Kelly got a nice gig out of coming to Buffalo, too. The young quarterback and new general manager were almost kindred spirits, both Irishmen and strong-willed. Kelly was seeking assurance that the Bills wanted to build a championship team. Polian vowed that Ralph Wilson was committed to building such a winner in Buffalo. "But we have to start with you," Polian told Kelly. "We have to get you first before we can do anything else."

Those negotiations became so heated, as Kelly writes in his autobiography, *Armed and Dangerous,* that they nearly exploded when his agent, A.J. Faigin, claimed that Kelly deserved a huge contract because he was going to take a beating at the expense of the Bills' weak offensive line. "Polian became enraged and challenged A.J. Faigin to drop down in front of him in a three-point stance," Kelly writes. "'If you know so much about offensive line play,' Polian growled, 'why don't you demonstrate the swim technique against a short-set formation for me? Come on!' A.J. took one look at Polian's face, which was red as his hair, and backed off."

Polian laughs about it now. "That's been exagerrated over the years," he said. "Just a typical agent and general manager by-play. The agent had made a disparaging remark."

Eventually they worked out a five-year, $8 million deal, which made Kelly the highest paid player in the game, an agreement that had been years in the making and had finally taken the quarterback down the Kensington Freeway into the heart of Buffalo. "If ever there was a quarterback made for a town and a team, it was Jim Kelly," Polian maintains to this day.

By the time he arrived at the Hilton Hotel for his first press conference as a Buffalo Bill, Kelly had to make his way through hundreds of fans who were chanting his name and cheering, "Go Bills" and "Super Bowl! Super Bowl!"

As far back as then. Right at the outset. Jim Kelly heard all about it.

It was all about the Super Bowl.

CHAPTER 3 | # Super Bowl XXV

THEY STILL HAD enough time. That's what Jim Kelly was think-ing with a shade more than two minutes remaining in Super Bowl XXV as he led the Bills back on the field one final time. There was just enough time to pull out another victory.

Kelly knew he had one timeout left and the two-minute warn-ing to help him finish off the New York Giants. And the 74,000 fans in Tampa Stadium knew the Bills didn't have to get all the way down the field, go 90 long yards for a touchdown. They were only down by one point. A field goal would win it.

This was the moment Kelly had longed for when he was grow-ing up in the small western Pennsylvania town of East Brady, root-ing for Penn State and the Pittsburgh Steelers. The Super Bowl Steelers had won four Super Bowls in six years when Kelly was a teenager back in the 1970s.

Now Kelly's time had come, and it was running out. The game was on the line. All eyes were on him. "Ever since I was a little boy, I wanted the ball in my hand, whether it was a basketball, baseball, or football," Kelly said. "I always wanted to be the guy to run the show. I thrived on it."

Only six weeks earlier, against these very same Giants, Kelly had been forced out of the game with an injury that threatened to end his season. For someone long accustomed to being the center of attention, few circumstances in football are more maddening than to be on the sideline, missing out on the action.

The injury occurred on a dank, overcast mid-December Saturday afternoon before a national television audience, when the Bills and Giants met with identical 11–2 records. It was a game that was hyped as the best of the AFC against the best of the NFC, maybe even a preview of the Super Bowl. Late in the first half with the Bills leading 14–10, Kelly directed a pass over the middle to Andre Reed, and when the quarterback hopped up on his toes to get a better look, he heard a pop in his left knee and he fell to the ground. It wasn't until much later that Kelly learned Will Wolford, his left tackle and bodyguard, had slammed into his knee, the result of a pinball collision with Giants linebacker Carl Banks and Buffalo left guard Jim Ritcher.

Bodies lay out on the turf. A season suddenly on the brink.

Now, with the Super Bowl in sight, Kelly found himself lying on the ground, experiencing the worst pain he had ever felt. But, to his surprise, the pain soon subsided, and he was able to get up and carefully and slowly make his way to the sideline without any assistance. Frank Reich took over at quarterback as Kelly attempted deep knee bends in front of the Buffalo bench, thinking he would be able to get right back out there. He just needed a couple of plays to compose himself, catch his breath, regain his strength. Then, feeling better and losing himself in the drama of the game, Kelly quickly jumped up on his toes to get a better view of a teammate's punt. Only this time, when he came down, his knee completely buckled. As he began to collapse, Howard Ballard, the enormous lineman all the Bills called "House," latched onto Kelly and held him upright.

Almost immediately Kelly grasped that there would be no gallant return to the gridiron on this day. While he did not know the full severity of the injury—that would be determined later with X-rays—he knew it was bad. Back in his USFL days, his other knee, his right knee, got banged up, but after a month of rest, he was ready to play again. He had avoided surgery that time. Now that was the best he could hope for as he was placed on a cart and driven to the locker room. The immediate diagnosis was a sprained medial collateral ligament with a prognosis of anywhere from two to six weeks for recovery. Two days later he would undergo an MRI that confirmed the initial evaluation.

Kelly wasn't the only quarterback to go down that day. Early in the second half after completing a short pass, Phil Simms was buried under the Buffalo defense and severely injured his right foot. Simms would be lost for the rest of the season, even if it extended to the last Sunday in January. Abruptly, the battle between two of the league's premier teams had taken a strange detour on the road to the Super Bowl. Jeff Hostetler replaced Simms just as Reich had done for Kelly, and the defenses took over and dominated as the understudies closed out the game.

Four times in the final quarter Buffalo's defenders turned back the Giants and held on for a 17–13 victory. But the Giants were not dismayed. They believed they had outplayed the Bills and had controlled the ball for 37 minutes and 59 seconds to Buffalo's 22 minutes and one second, an ominous harbinger of what was to come in the Super Bowl.

"That game in the Meadowlands was a very hard-fought game," Bill Parcells recalled years later. "And we got behind early in that game and we had a little trouble with the no-huddle, the tempo and speed of it. It took a little getting used to for us. And we played better as the game went on, but we didn't have quite enough to beat them that day. After we had come back and made it close, they ran the clock out on us, making a couple of first downs where I thought we would get at least one more possession. "What I will tell you about that game that served us well in the Super Bowl, if you go back and look at the statistics of that game, [is that] we really controlled the game pretty well in New York. We rushed for, I don't know, close to 160 yards. We held them down to something 200 yards and 17 points."

Through an unusual scheduling quirk, that December game in the Meadowlands was actually the second time the teams had met that year. In the summer, during the preseason, they played in Buffalo. "Coach Levy approached the preseason games quite differently than we did," Parcells said. "He didn't play his regulars quite as much. And we had some pretty young guys. I remember Rodney Hampton was a rookie tailback that we had, and so we tried to put a little more emphasis on the game than they did. I'm certain we did."

But what Parcells took from that game was that "we ran the ball extremely well that night in the preseason." And that would serve as his game plan for the battles that would ensue in December and January.

In the NFC Championship Game, which was played in San Francisco, the Giants survived a brutal confrontation with a 49ers team vying for an unprecedented third straight Super Bowl title. Joe Montana was knocked out of the game and, with Hostetler at quarterback, the Giants managed to win 15–13 on Matt Bahr's fifth and final field goal as the game ended. "That was a hotly contested, physical game," Parcells remembered. "But again it was an opponent we had played in the regular season, and we knew about them. We had been playing San Francisco a lot through the years, starting in '84, '85, '86, through '90. We had been playing them quite a bit, so their key players we were familiar with, much like those three games with Buffalo in '90. We knew a lot about their players."

As his team got ready to take the field against the Niners for the NFC championship, Parcells was aware that the Bills had already routed the Los Angeles Raiders 51–3. "That score was very surprising to me," he remembered. "That game has to be one of the greatest games any team under those circumstances had ever played. I can't ever remember a game more one-sided with an AFC or an NFC championship on the line. Winning the game by 48 points, that's impressive."

As they made their way to Tampa for the Super Bowl, the Giants knew they had passed one huge roadblock in the tournament. "We had been slugging it out with San Francisco over the years so we knew that game wasn't going to be much different" Parcells said. "We had been in enough of those games—three, four-point games—with San Francisco in recent years leading up to '90 that we knew it was going to be a tough assignment."

There would be no week off before this Super Bowl. Players would have less time to heal and coaches less time to prepare. Luckily both the Bills and Giants were familiar with each other's personnel and tendencies. "Both teams were pretty happy to being playing one another because by playing the Bills we're playing a team we're familiar with and vice versa," Parcells said. "So that's a little bit of a break. You know it's a coincidence that doesn't occur very often, playing a team in the regular season but not only that, playing the team in the preseason. And now you're playing them for the world championship, and that doesn't happen very often. So in some ways that was an advantage for us in terms of preparation and how we're going to approach the game. Our whole coaching staff knew pretty much what we had to do to beat these guys, and I'm sure Buffalo really knew by that time what we were going to try to do."

Without a doubt, as they prepared for the Super Bowl, Parcells and his coaching staff knew they could not win a high-scoring game with the Bills. "If we were going to get into a shootout with Buffalo, we were going to get beat," he said. "I remember saying, 'These guys are pretty dynamic. If we get behind in this game, a few scores behind in this game, there's probably a good chance we're going to have trouble catching them. They're dynamic when they get the lead and they get more and more aggressive.' So I said a way we have to approach them is if you look at the preseason, we ran the ball well; if you look at the regular season, we ran the ball well. We need to try and shorten this game as far as their offense goes. And that was pretty much the whole thing for us. We had a big back in Ottis Anderson and we had two tremendous blockers on the left side, Jumbo Elliott and Mark Bavaro—and they were very important players in the game. And, of course, [we were] playing with Jeff Hostetler, who only had four or five games of experience because he hadn't been a starter until Phil Simms got hurt in that first Buffalo game in December."

After that loss in December, Lawrence Taylor, the great Giants outside linebacker, said with disdain, "We shouldn't have lost that game. They're a fine team and all, but when Kelly went out, it took the air out of their balloons. You could see that."

Asked if he could see the Bills making it to the Super Bowl, Steve DeOssie, another Giants linebacker, took a moment before declaring, "Yeah, I could see them in the Super Bowl. And I'd like to see them from across the field."

So there they were again, with the final minutes of the season winding down. The Bills needed to move the ball—maybe 60 yards would be just enough—into field goal range for Scott Norwood. It was up to Kelly to get them there. He had been in so many similar situations, from his high schools days in Pennsylvania and his time at the University of Miami to so many wild shootouts in the USFL and even on several occasions with the Bills against the best defensive players in the NFL. "You get paid to deliver in the big moments," Kelly said. "That's what it's all about."

Perhaps the pivotal moment in the Bills' rise to prominence had come in the previous season's opening game down in Miami, when Kelly led two touchdown drives in the final five minutes to finally end Buffalo's 20-game losing streak to Don Shula's team. Trailing 24–13 in the early-September heat of the Orange Bowl, Kelly completed five straight passes, including a 26-yard strike for a touchdown, to get the Bills back in contention. Then, with less than two minutes remaining, Kelly took them 49 yards downfield to win the game. He did it with his arm—connecting on five more passes—and his legs—dropping back to pass from the 2-yard line and suddenly deciding to run for the end zone and the winning score with two seconds left.

"The famous game in Miami," is how Bill Polian refers to it. "Coach Shula was in his prime, and they were the top of the league with Marino and [Mark] Clayton and [Mark] Duper. It was a beautiful hot day, and we take the ball down the field and we're on the 4-yard line and Marv called a draw. I think Jim may have told [center] Kent Hull, but he didn't tell anybody else. So he keeps the ball and runs up the middle and makes it over the goal line. Of course, I was in the press box, so I could see that he made it over, but there was some hesitation on the part of the officials, and then they signaled touchdown, and the bench empties, and Jim's in the bottom of a pile of 53 guys celebrating wildly because we had finally broken the Dolphins jinx. And he said afterward that he was really worried that he couldn't breathe.

"And that was the first time, I recall, the first of many times, that there was a big group of fans to greet us when we got back. And the fact that we had broken the Dolphins jinx and he did it on a play that he decided, *I'm going to take this on my shoulders to win the game*. That's Jim Kelly."

Kelly's true grit won the admiration and trust of his teammates and fans. "He was a tough guy. He wasn't a prima donna quarterback," safety Mark Kelso said. "He'd just as soon put his shoulder down and run you over when he could run—not that he was the swiftest guy when got out of that pocket. But he could certainly take a lot of hits and had a tremendous amount of toughness, and I think he was quintessential Buffalo."

"It didn't matter how many touchdowns we were behind in Miami," Ritcher remembered. "We came back and won that game in the fourth quarter, and the whole team started to build from that time on. Got to give Jim a lot of the credit for turning us around. That's just the way he is, the general—the way he'd lead."

In the second month of the 1990 season, Kelly brought the Bills back with late-game scoring drives to beat the Denver Broncos, Raiders, and New York Jets in consecutive weeks. It established them as a team that could make big plays, handle pressure, and overcome adversity. "They pay the quarterback big money to bring you back at times like that," Kelly said. "There are going to be times like that when things don't go the way you want, but what matters is what you do about them, how you turn those negatives into positives. Being a leader, you have to find a way to get it done."

If leadership was built around attitude, it was an attribute Kelly had in abundance. Something beyond confidence. A kind of cocky arrogance. I'm better than you. Just gimme the ball. It was a force field that changed the Buffalo Bills. "Jim had a huge ego that first year or two." Bob Koshinski said. "And then you brought in Thurman Thomas, who had a chip on his shoulder. And Bruce Smith was already there and Bruce was a me guy."

"When Jim came in, he arrived with such an attitude that we didn't have in the past," Ritcher said. *"Just give me some time and we can win this ball game. Just give me the ball and we'll get down the field.* I think before he came in, we had some great ballplayers on our team, but we maybe felt a little snakebit. We'd go out there and be playing well and be ahead, and then one bad thing would happen, and we'd all look at each other and go, 'Oh, wow. Here it comes, man.' Like we were snakebit. And Jim wouldn't let us feel that way. He'd never let us feel sorry for ourselves. It was always 'Keep fighting.' Always 'Give me some time, give me a chance.'"

Finally, in the 1990 season Kelly, and his Bills, had the chance of a lifetime. It was only a matter of time. Throughout the season scoring had never been a problem for the Bills. At least not until the final night of the season. In their previous two playoff games, they had put up 95 points and looked unstoppable, which is why oddsmakers made Buffalo a seven-point favorite to defeat the Giants.

Just the week before, the Bills had hung up 51 on the Raiders, 41 in the first half, basically closing out the game on cruise control.

That game was marked by Kelly's return and coincided with the absence of Bo Jackson from the Raiders backfield. One of the greatest athletes of his time, Jackson felt his hip come out of its socket when he was tackled in the previous week's playoff game against the Cincinnati Bengals. Despite lying on the turf in considerable pain, what the rest of us would call unbearable pain, Bo managed to pop his hip back into place with about as much effort as when he would shatter a baseball bat over his thigh. This was beyond the theater of the absurd, even for an athlete who could do almost anything on a field. Although Bo would never play football again, he was able to resume his baseball career. George Brett, Bo's Hall of Fame teammate on the Kansas City Royals who had attended that playoff game, asked the Raiders' trainer, George Anderson, if Bo really had popped his hip back into place. His answer: "That's just impossible. No one's that strong."

Without Bo for the AFC Championship Game, the Raiders turned to Marcus Allen—the Most Valuable Player of Super Bowl XVIII, who averaged 5.4 yards per carry in his playoff career—to get them to Tampa. It was not to be. The Raiders were simply overmatched and overcome by the Bills.

Dennis DiPaolo will never forget what came next: Tampa. The Super Bowl. "It was so exciting. Your heart was pumping as soon as you got in the Tampa airport and saw all your Buffalo logos hanging everywhere," he said. "All our colors. Everywhere you went you'd see our colors. Everywhere you went it was, 'Go Bills.' The excitement was just phenomenal. The hotel we stayed at, the code word was 'Cumpa,' which in Italian means compare. It means everybody's equal. We stayed there with the Bills the whole time. It was like everybody really was part of the team."

Koshinski and representatives from all the TV stations and newspapers in upstate New York flew into Tampa to cover the biggest sporting event in Buffalo's history. "I remember that first Monday night when they landed in Tampa, and we were outside their hotel, and they got off the bus and they greeted some of the fans who were going crazy," Koshinski said. "More than one of those players coming off the bus was inebriated. I mean, they had partied for 24 hours! In Buffalo you still hear these rumors to this day that players were out drinking the night before the Super Bowl, and they were seen at five in the morning staggering out of a bar. That's all nonsense. You know, Polian had that team under wraps."

It was a short, intense week that didn't afford any time for an extended celebration after winning the conference championship. Security was heightened all around Tampa because of the war in Iraq. "So that put a different light on things," Polian says. "You recognized that there are far more important things in the world than a football game, even a Super Bowl. Still, what it meant for everybody in western New York was: we've finally reached the pinnacle after the depths that we had been in. It was just an incredible experience to recognize all the euphoria that surrounded it."

For Pete Metzelaars, everything seemed rushed for that first Super Bowl. "The first Super Bowl week was kind of chaotic," he said. "We only had a week between the championship game and the Super Bowl. It was our first Super Bowl, so everything was just a little out of control with flights for our families. 'Who's got enough tickets? Where's everybody staying?' My wife, Barbara, did an unbelievable job taking care of all that kind of stuff with the Bills. It all happened so fast. So it was a huge thing getting everybody there."

On Tuesday morning, when the team buses pulled out of the airport's Holiday Inn, Polian rode with the players for picture day, and as they turned onto North Dale Mabry Highway, Tampa Stadium came into view. Jeff Wright, the nose tackle, turned to Polian and said, "Holy shit, Bill. We're in the Super Bowl." The general manager could only laugh and say, "Jeff you're exactly right."

"That captured the moment," Polian said years later. "I knew exactly what he meant. When you look back on it and try to put it into perspective, from the time you're 10 years old you dream of being in that game if you're a football player, and all of a sudden you're there. It's a breathtaking experience."

"Before you knew it, it was time to play the game," Metzelaars said.

But the game did not go according to the Bills' game plan. "I think what really did them in was they won so convincingly over the Raiders," Koshinski said. "It was a short week. They had already beaten the Giants in December. They were playing so well. I don't think they really thought there was a chance they were going to lose that game."

If the Bills appeared to be on a stampede, the Giants were only too eager to corral them. On this night, the first time a Super Bowl had begun in the evening, at a little past 6:00 in Tampa, the Giants had frustrated the Bills with a variety of defensive schemes that stymied Kelly and his receivers. Although Kelly had been able to connect with Reed early in the first quarter, a tipped pass that went for 61 yards all the way to the Giants 8-yard line, the drive immediately stalled. It was an indication that things were not going to come easily for Kelly and his teammates. The Bills were forced to settle for a chip-shot field goal from Norwood that tied the game. Still, that early strike to Reed encouraged Kelly to keep "looking for the home-run ball" all night, "and that's usually when a quarterback begins hurting his performance," he later acknowledged.

The Giants had employed a risky and imaginative defensive game plan to disrupt the Bills wide-open attack. From the start what Coach Parcells and defensive coordinator Bill Belichick really threw at Kelly was the kind of prevent defense you normally see at the end of a game, when a team is nursing a comfortable lead and victory is assured. From the very first series of downs, the Giants had come out with two down linemen and five linebackers, and dropped six, sometimes seven men back into pass coverage as they began to relentlessly hound and pound Buffalo's receivers all night long. It was football's version of the rope-a-dope.

When the analogy was mentioned to Parcells more than 20 years later, he said, "I agree with that. A matchup we were afraid of, you know we had to worry about Lofton because of his speed. We knew Reed was going to be inside there quite a bit and we felt we had to hit him hard and we really crunched that. But the matchup we were really worried about was Thurman. We were really trying to use what actually Bill Belichick went on to use for years, a technique against Marshall Faulk when the Patriots beat the Rams for the Super Bowl. What we call 'the Butch Technique,' where the defensive end rushes and tries to chip off that halfback as he rushes, or an outside linebacker, whichever the case may be. And so we were trying to do that to Thurman almost every time on the rush to try and knock him off stride, knock him off balance, and that's become a popular thing to do on good pass-receiving backs."

"The Giants' attitude was, 'Fine, throw the ball. We're just going to kill your receivers,'" Kelly remembered. "It's tough enough for any receiver to catch the ball over the middle. But having two linebackers waiting there to drill him is a hell of a lot tougher than dealing with two safeties."

Kelly was no different from any other big-armed, big-time quarterback. They all loved to throw long, stretch the field, flex their muscles, and strut their stuff. They all yearned to be the chosen one with the ball in their hands, the game on the line, the clock winding down, ready to deliver the knockout punch. And they all knew no one had a gun quite like Dan Marino, the great Miami quarterback. They all marveled at the way Marino could pile up miles upon miles of yardage. Dan was the man, the man with the golden arm, whom they all held in awe. At celebrity fund-raisers or golf outings, on those rare occasions when all the elite quarterbacks would all get together and sit around and drink and discuss their craft, Marino was the one they most sought out, the one who held the key to football's holy grail, the one who was blessed with a god-given cannon for an arm. With a flinch of his shoulder, Marino could freeze a defense, or fool them with a pump of his right arm and leave them utterly defenseless all the way down the field. Marino could do this better than anyone they had ever seen throw a football. He was the template. He was the man.

Now Kelly had the golden opportunity to show the world that *he* was that man. That he was as good as any of them who had come out of the class of 1983 and that incredible draft—including Marino. That he could be the first one from that celebrated group to lead his team to a Super Bowl win. With the players around him, Kelly knew he could make this comeback, that he possessed that special gift. "I wasn't stupid. I knew we had Thurman Thomas in the backfield, and James Lofton and Andre Reed. And the offensive line was really good," Kelly said. "I took every snap from my center Kent Hull. I just had to keep my game under control."

As far back as he could remember, Kelly always liked the fast pace of the game. His mother would tell him to slow down, but Jim always liked to be on the move. When the Bills began to go with a no-huddle offense, a hurry-up offense that made it difficult for defenses to substitute players and make adjustments, it was quickly dubbed the K-Gun. Although most fans assumed it was named for Kelly, it was, in fact, a moniker for Keith McKeller, the tight end who would enter the game and complement the Bills' three wide receivers.

The K-Gun let everyone know the Bills were going to quicken the pace, change the tempo of the game, and throw the ball, and it required great discipline and skill from Kelly. The quarterback needed the intelligence to call the right plays from the line of scrimmage and an inherent ability to maintain a sense of calm that would enable him to perform without a moment's hesitation. When the K-Gun was clicking, it was not uncommon for the Bills to drive 80 yards for a touchdown with a couple of quick strikes.

Although the K-Gun seemed innovative when the Bills began utilizing it in the late '80s, some of its seeds had been planted in the USFL when Kelly studied under Houston Gamblers offensive coordinator Darrell "Mouse" Davis. Mouse liked to play groundbreaking football, football played on a fast track, which played right into Kelly's strengths. This new thing called "run and shoot,"—well, at first Kelly had no idea what Mouse was talking about. But he learned fast.

It didn't hurt Kelly's development that he began his professional career in the USFL, just as it didn't hurt Joe Namath that he began his career in the American Football League. New leagues are open to new ideas and new ways to attract attention and create a following. So Kelly couldn't have been happier starting out in Texas, where football is a kind of religion, even if it was with an unknown outfit. Kelly was encouraged, instructed was more like it, to throw 40 or 50 times a game. What quarterback wouldn't love that?

"It was a blast," Kelly recalled. "Mouse really taught me the passing game and he really worked on my footwork. In order to be in the run-and-shoot offense, you have to have quick feet. When I came out of college, I had blown my shoulder out—I never played my senior year except for three games. A lot of teams, I mean Buffalo took a chance drafting me, because here's a quarterback that had three metal rods sticking out of his arm. I was told I'd never throw the ball again. That's a big chance. But Mouse stayed with me. He worked on my footwork and got me ready to play, and I put up 83 touchdowns and 10,000 yards in two years."

The run-and-shoot had morphed into a hurry-up, no-huddle offense, and for Kelly, a self-proclaimed "likes to do things quick," it was the ideal way to attack defenses.

"People couldn't handle our K-Gun," said Jim Ritcher. "We'd just leave our five linemen to pick up whoever they brought, whoever they rushed. And Buddy Ryan, one of the great defensive minds, just didn't believe when he was coaching Philadelphia that five guys were going to be able to withstand as many blitzes as we thought we could handle. Buddy was a big talker and said Kelly was going to get hurt in that game. And the first three drives, I don't remember if we scored three touchdowns, but we kept moving the ball and scoring, and they finally stopped bringing all those blitzes. They might get a hit on Kelly, but that ball was going to be thrown."

It's no wonder Kelly had entered the Super Bowl briming with confidence. He had just orchestrated a half dozen touchdown drives against one the of the best defenses in football, the Raiders, that covered 57 to 78 yards. "The way I look at it," he proclaimed after that performance, "we can only stop ourselves. We've got so much talent. Getting one week to prepare for us, instead of two, is the best thing that could happen to us. We're on a roll, playing great ball. We're ready to go."

But in the Super Bowl, in their rematch with the Giants, the Bills had to scratch and claw for practically every yard they gained. Confronted by the defensive brain trust of two other Bills, Parcells and Belichick, the Buffalo offense was stymied. And the frustration only kept building in Kelly as the night wore on. There was little Kelly could do about it. The Giants had two long, time-consuming touchdown drives that bridged the end of the first half and opening of the second half; all the Bills offense could do was stand around and wait to get their hands on the ball again. "We had pretty much one way to approach the game," Parcells fondly recalled, "and that was to shorten the game, control the ball. We made some outstanding long drives in that game that kept their offense on the bench, particularly at the end of the half and then right at the start of the third quarter. Those were the two most notable drives."

"There was like an hour and a half where it felt we were on the sideline, never hit the field," Kelly said. "I mean, right before the half they had the football and they marched on for eight or nine minutes with the ball. *Boom,* halftime. Then you go through that long halftime, and then we kick off to them, and they get the ball and they control the clock again, and they come down, I don't even know, probably a good hour, hour and a half, that we weren't even on the football field. If I look back on any regrets that I ever have, probably I would be more patient and maybe try to run the ball a little bit more than we did."

But running the ball was not always Kelly's call. The plays were being called from the sideline by the coaches who, frustrated as well, kept pursuing the big play, going for the big score. Late in the third quarter, the Bills were facing third down and a very short yard, when the call came for a play-action pass that fell incomplete.

When Ritcher came to the sideline, he asked assistant coach Tom Bresnahan, "'How come we didn't run the ball on that? It was real short,'" Ritcher recalled. "And he said, 'We thought it was a lot longer than it was.' I thought, 'Uh, big mistake there.' But you can't blame 'em. They thought it was a lot longer."

As they had in the game back in December, the Giants held the ball longer—much, much longer—severely limiting Buffalo's time of possession. Kelly couldn't help calculating, "When you only have 19 minutes with the football, we scored a point a minute."

A point a minute. They had been scoring nearly like that before they got to Tampa! And a point a minute almost looked like it might hold up when Thurman Thomas bolted 31 yards into the end zone to give Buffalo a 19–17 advantage at the outset of the fourth quarter. But the Giants bounced back and took a 20–19 lead on a short Bahr field goal. "We had a chance to put the game away down near the goal line in the fourth quarter," Parcells said, "and we had to settle for a field goal there because a player named Jeff Wright. I'll never forget this. He made an outstanding play. He ran behind our center Bart Oates. I mean, Oates had position on him so well, and Wright went totally behind him and still was able to make the tackle on Ottis Anderson in the backfield. That was the single biggest play in the game that gave Buffalo a chance to win the game."

Thanks to Jeff Wright, the Bills would not have to drive the entire length of the field to score a touchdown to win the game. A field goal would do it.

But Buffalo still had to beat the clock. The Giants had controlled the ball for 40 minutes and 33 seconds. Only two minutes and 16 seconds remained—still enough time for Kelly to position Buffalo for its first title since 1965 when Jack Kemp and Cookie Gilchrist were playing in the old American Football League, and this western New York industrial city began to embrace its team, and long before there ever was a championship game called the Super Bowl.

Polian was down on the field now, ready to watch the team he had built put the finishing touches on a season that would bring Buffalo its first true world championship. For most of the evening, Polian had watched the game from the press box, where two seats had been set aside for the general managers of each team, Polian and George Young of the Giants. "In those days the league made no accommodations or minimal accommodations for the administrative staff of the competing teams," Polian recalled. "And we have five people sit together on gameday, senior administrators, so we started watching the game from the roof of the press box. But because of the security precautions with the war they had SWAT teams up there, so there wasn't a lot of room. So we wound up going down to the press box to grab whatever seats or standing room we could. I got to sit throughout the game, but it was kind of touch and go. It was not the normal situation."

Late in the game, with the outcome clearly undecided, a league official ushered the two general managers down to the field so they would have quick access to their team's locker room where the Vince Lombardi Trophy presentation would take place.

As his team huddled one last time near the goal line, Polian was confident of the outcome. "We're going to have one last drive to win it," he remembered thinking. "You know how many times Jim Kelly had one last drive to win it and won. So I think everybody said, this is where we want to be. So the game's going to come down to this and not only do we like our chances, we believe we'll do it."

For Kelly it was everything he had been dreaming about his whole life. It was the ultimate challenge of his career. Shoot out the lights on the Giants. "To be a leader, one of the things you need to do is win games you're not supposed to win," Kelly says. "And you need to come back when you need to. It doesn't matter what the circumstances are, what the conditions are. There are going to be times when things are not going to go well, when they don't go the way you want, but it's what you do about it that counts. My father used to teach us that."

All those life lessons his father would tell him about as a young boy at the dinner table back in East Brady, Pennsylvania, with his five brothers and his mother crowded around the kitchen had come to fruition. "You have to turn those negatives into positives," the son remembered. "You have to make a situation better. Find a way to get it done."

If only the Bills could get the ball within striking distance for Norwood, the night would finally belong to them. The ball was on the Buffalo 10-yard line, the Giants end zone was 90 yards away. The Bills needed to reach the Giants 30-yard line if Norwood would have a realistic chance of coming through. Although he had kicked one from 48 yards back in September, he had missed on four tries from beyond the 40-yard line during the season.

But what no one on the Bills sideline really wanted to remember was that his longest field goal of the year came on the artificial turf at Giants Stadium against the Jets. A surface far more supportive for kickers.

Norwood was warming up on the sidelines, anxious to get back on the field and win the game. Reich, who would hold the ball for Norwood's kick, was only concerned about Kelly and the game at hand. "I'm watching the offense," Reich remembered. "Jim's out there doing his thing. We always had a little thing going on where he knew I was on the sideline and we had a signaling system where if he wanted to look at me for an idea or two I'd be there, so I gotta be tuned in to what the offense is doing. The other thing is he could go down on any play. So I'm not concerned with kicking the field goal. I'm focused on what the offense is doing."

The ball and the game were in Kelly's hands. As Kelly went back to pass, a few yards from his own end zone, he was again forced to scramble his way out of trouble, as he had so many times throughout the night. Finally, on their third play, third-and-inches from their 19-yard line, Thurman Thomas burst through the left side for 22 yards. Suddenly the Bills were on the move.

"The whole drive, time was flying so fast," Metzelaars remembered. "It seemed like the whole game lasted 15, 20 minutes. It was like at warp speed. Everything just happened so fast. Getting down, getting back to run another play. We were running the ball, completing a couple of passes. Thurman was running the ball like crazy. We thought we had a great chance."

After a short completion to Reed, Kelly once again dropped back to pass and was forced to run, this time breaking away for 9 yards and a first down at the Giants 46-yard line. Buffalo took its final timeout with 48 seconds on the clock. On the sideline,

Norwood kept kicking into a net, working on his stroke, getting his rhythm and timing just right, his confidence building and his heart pounding as the Bills kept advancing down the field.

With 29 seconds left the Bills caught a break: the video replay official needed a timeout to review a six-yard shoestring catch by the tight end Keith McKeller at the Giants 40-yard line.

All around him Polian could see "there was a lot of confusion going on because of the replay review. And Marv turned around and saw me and I smiled and said, 'Well, you've got to give Jim a play.' So Marv got everybody together, and I believe Ted [Marchibroda, the offensive coordinator] called the play, and it was a draw. And Marv said, 'Remember to tell Thurman to get out of bounds, that we don't have a timeout remaining.'"

It was an inspired and risky call, on second-and-4 from the Giants 40-yard line. If Thomas was stopped for a short gain or could not get out of bounds, the Bills would be forced to try a desperate Hail Mary pass or set up hastily for an extremely long field-goal attempt.

On the seventh play of the drive, Thomas picked up valuable yardage, as he had all night, swinging out toward the right sideline. Then, with Mark Collins sealing the corner, Thomas cut back in a flash, where there was an opening. He headed for the end zone before Collins lunged, grabbing him around the waist and bringing him down on the 29-yard line.

It had been a risky and valiant run. He had gained 11 vital yards on his 15th and final carry of the night and he had piled up 135 yards in the game. But he did not get out of bounds. And time was slipping away.

Kelly immediately spiked the ball to stop the clock.

When the drive began, Parcells calculated how far the Bills needed to go to have a makeable field goal. "I generally feel like 35, maybe 33 yards to have a shot at it," he reemembered. "Somewhere near where they got." And then his mind travels back to Thomas' final run and the play his cornerbacks made. "We made a little defensive mistake late in the game. Not a mistake on the field, a mistake strategically. And Thurman made that run right there at the end, and we really had six defensive backs in passing defense. It was a very gutsy call by Buffalo, but it gave them a chance to win the game."

Reminded the Bills had no timeouts left, Parcells said, "Yes, it was a very gutsy call. You know, I remember Bill Belichick and I, we talked about that right at that time. I said, 'We might have made a mistake there, Bill.' And those are the kind of things that can cost you. I think strategically it was a very good play by Buffalo and certainly caught us by surprise."

Eight seconds remained. The game was out of Kelly's hands now. His night's work was over. Kelly unfastened his chin strap and headed to the sideline, where he stood next to his teammates to watch the end of the game. His heart was still pounding, and there was nothing more for him to do but wait and watch.

The football was nestled just inside the 30-yard line, just where Kelly and the Bills believed they needed to get it as Scott Norwood made his way onto the field to end the game.

CHAPTER 4 | Eight Seconds of Infamy

N THE WEDNESDAY before the Super Bowl, a reporter asked Scott Norwood if the game were to be decided by a last second kick, did it mean anything that Buffalo had routed the Raiders while the Giants just survived on Matt Bahr's last-second, game-winning field goal over the 49ers. "Well," Norwood began, trying to shrug off the question. "Like Matt said after that one, 'You're only as good as your next kick.' I think I'm prepared for anything. But the way the offense has been going, I don't expect that kind of finish."

It was another game of football—soccer, as it is known around the world—that Norwood "picked up early at about six or seven years old." He recalls being "self-taught, with a natural soccer-style swing." His father, Del, was a successful high school soccer and baseball coach for 30 years who was inducted into the Virginia High School Sports Hall of Fame. He "was always there," Norwood said, "always went to the field with me when he could, always supported me." By the time Scott entered Thomas Jefferson High School in Alexandria, Virginia, Scott was an accomplished sweeper who was twice named to the All-Metropolitan team.

Then one afternoon another high school coach, Jefferson's football coach, Mike Weaver, approached the 17-year old leaving soccer practice. "Son, I hear you can really kick the ball," said the coach.

"I'm okay, sir."

"We need a kicker, son," Weaver told the stocky, 5'10" kid who seemed to have magic in his leg. "Why don't you come out for the team this season?"

It was something Norwood had never really considered before. Soccer had consumed his interest. But that night at dinner, he discussed it with his father, who simply asked his son if this was something he wanted to pursue. "You know," Scott recalled, "I think I do."

That summer, as the story was documented in *Sports Illustrated*, Del helped his son any way he could. He held the ball as Scott kicked. He shagged kickoffs. He drilled his son on the fundamentals of kicking a football over and over again. He offered advice when his kicks went off line. "Nothing heavy-handed," Norwood said. "Subtle suggestions. Always 'think about the moment, not what's happened in the past. Do the best with what you're faced with. Be confident.'"

His father taught him to always maintain a calm demeanor and focus and tried to instill the confidence to back up all that natural ability his son possessed. He also encouraged his son never to get down on himself, to always remain upbeat against the strong currents of adversity that were certain to confront a kicker and would surely one day end up kicking him in the face. In his way, he was preparing his son for nothing less than success.

And success came quickly, as it so often does with natural athletes. Following his senior year of high school, Scott earned an athletic scholarship to James Madison University. But it wasn't until after college that Scott encountered some of the hard knocks that all football players must endure. He was cut by the Atlanta Falcons, but even the pain of this setback was quickly relieved when he latched on with the Birmingham Stallions of the USFL. Then, in his second professional season, he tore some cartilage in his knee and was cast away again.

Refusing to believe that his career was over, he returned to the place where it all began: the high school field where he spent that long, hot summer with his dad before his final year of high school, sharpening his stroke, convinced he would get another shot with another team, somewhere out there. From seemingly out of nowhere the call came from Buffalo. They were auditioning kickers. The way it was phrased, it almost sounded like a chorus line for some Broadway show.

Norwood was one of 10 men brought into camp. Then, near the end of training camp, Norwood looked around and found he didn't see any other kickers on the field. Bill Polian came over to him, extended his hand, and said, "Congratulations. It was a pretty clear decision. You had the best camp here."

Maybe a thrill like that only comes once in a lifetime. Only now, in Super Bowl XXV, Norwood was trotting out the middle of the field with a Super Bowl win riding on his foot. It was moment for which he had been preparing for several years. "You always think in a big game like that that you'll play a large role in it, play an important part. That's what you always prepare for. In practice you always make each kick very important," Norwood said.

As Norwood took the field, he knew the ball would be set on the grass at the 37-yard line. From that distance, a kicker will fail more than 50 percent of the time. Maybe you break even. Maybe you break everything down too much. You get 1.3 seconds to make your kick and leave your mark on the game.

Just 1.3 seconds.

An eternity.

Adam Lingner will snap the ball, Frank Reich will place it down, and the rest is up to Norwood.

Eight seconds on the game clock.

As he kneels down to take his position, Frank Reich says nothing to Norwood. He barely looks at Norwood a few feet behind him. "Scott's going to give you a spot," Reich remembered years later. "We kinda had a rhythm and a cadence to it back then. Nothing special. It all happens pretty quick."

One point three seconds.

"Everything is about giving the kicker a long look at the ball, a steady look," Reich explained. "Just do what you do in practice."

Do you pat the grass? Smooth out any rough patch of dirt?

"No," Reich says. "You want to be innocuous. You don't want to draw any attention to yourself. You just want to get your job done. You want to play down the moment. You don't want anyone in the world to even know you exist."

All over the world fans are watching.

The air appears to be still. No strong winds or currents to deal with. Everything is nice and calm. In Norwood's world there is no crowd; all sound is blocked out. *Just keep your head down and kick. Nothing to it. You've been doing it all your life.*

"You want to leave Scott alone," Reich said. "I'm absolutely thinking that we're going to win the Super Bowl. I'm thinking this is a huge moment for Buffalo. This is our first Super Bowl, and I'm thinking we're going to win it."

From the moment the Bills began their final drive, Norwood had been kicking into a net along the sidelines, practicing with the cadence and rhythm of his inner metronome, the way he had been taught to approach the ball from the place where it will be held: three steps back and two to the left.

He had made game-winning kicks before, but that was not on his mind now, not with eight seconds remaining on the biggest stage in American sports. He was locked in on the distance and the powerful kick he would need to unleash. "I wanted to get it off fast and I wanted to get it high so it wouldn't get blocked," he said. "I wanted to hit the ball solid."

"Most kickers want to kick it in one point three seconds," Reich said. "Scott was a little bit faster than that."

Suddenly Norwood was afforded even more time to review the mechanics of his craft, step by step, every inch of the way, the moment that would forever define his career. The Giants had called timeout to freeze Norwood. "You got nothing left there but that," Parcells remembered of using that final timeout—just as his own field goal kickers rushed up to him. "I have two field goal kickers there," Parcells said. "Matt Bahr, who was a pretty astute guy, and Raul Allegre, who had been on injured reserve for us. And they both came to me prior to the kick and they both said the same thing. Matt was the first to say, 'Bill, he hasn't made one 47 yards on grass all year.' And Matt Bahr told me there's a good chance he'll try and overkick this ball."

But Parcells' immediate focus was on his unit on the field, hoping they might somehow block the kick. "I'm just looking to our defensive field goal team because I desperately don't want an offside penalty," he remembered. "So I know we had mentioned that to them. That's what I was looking at, and to see if we got anybody free off the corner who has a good shot at it. You know, that grass field was a little slow, and it's hard to get to those field goals and extra points on a field surface like that. So we try to push hard in the middle, hard off the corner on one side, and that's the best we can do. I just hoped we stayed onside."

All the Bills and Norwood could do was stand around and wait and, of course, unwittingly consider the magnitude of the moment, the enormity of the situation, the one shot at immortality. "You have to stand around for a couple of minutes," Norwood said. "The old ice-the-kicker. But it also gives the kicker a chance to get relaxed out there, consider the variables. I'm sure things kind of broke down in some sense because of that. I think the magnitude of the kick would have to weigh on anybody in that situation. I think no kicker's probably felt the pressure of a kick of that magnitude. Primarily the situation as well as the distance, the two factors combined, made it a tough one but certainly makeable. Still, I was very positive I could make the kick. You always expect to make it."

Both sides of the field were lined with players standing at attention, the way so many of them had hours before the game began when an inspiring flyover by a convoy of Air Force jets honoring the American forces in the Persian Gulf War had sailed over the stadium for all the world to behold. Now most of the Bills, and just as many Giants, were holding hands, many in silent prayer, as Norwood waited for the snap.

Polian, who was standing alongside his players, recalls the wind "blowing slightly" and a member of his front-office staff saying, "Boy, this is tough."

"No," Polian told him, "Scotty will make this. No sweat."

There was however, considerable cause for concern. Norwood's career had been in steady decline. His field goal percentage had dropped from 86.5 percent to 77 percent to 69 percent in the past three seasons.

Mark Kelso, the safety who roomed with Norwood on road trips, experienced an odd sensation as he awaited the kick. "It was ironic because you have Bills players and Giants players on the sideline saying prayers and holding hands, hoping to win. And the previous week the Giants are praying for Bahr to make a field goal to beat the 49ers and now they're praying for a missed field goal to win," he said.

Jim Kelly "was confident he was going to put it through. I saw him warming up before the game, and even though it was on grass, I felt he was good within 50 yards. I just was confident he was going knock it through, and we'd all go home happy," he said.

To compensate for the stillness of the night, Reich now remembers the way Norwood had practiced right before the game: "In the pregame warm-up I thought Scott was hooking the ball a little bit more than normal."

Back in Buffalo, like so many other Bills fans, Ange Coniglio had been waiting on this moment for what seemed like a lifetime. He was at a party, "and we're doing the same things the players were doing," he said. "We're holding hands. What can I tell you other than it was the culmination of something we had waited for a long time, sort of breathless. Maybe 20 people there waiting, praying."

His nephew, Bob Coniglio, was at his fraternity house, Sigma Alpha Mu, on the University of Buffalo campus. "About 85 percent of the kids were from Long Island and New York City. They were big Giants fans," he said. "I remember we had two TVs going. One room was all Bills fans, and the other room was all Giants fans. And we're holding hands in one room just like the Bills were, hoping the kick would go through."

Dennis DiPaolo was seated on the 40-yard line. "The Bills always took care of us," he said. "Back in the '60s, we started our restaurant, and the Bills were just starting, and my father was the main headliner in town, the pro wrestler. Pro wrestling and boxing were big things in Buffalo back in the '50s and early '60s. So we always had a special relationship with the Bills. And when we talk about Buffalo, we can't even imagine the city surviving if we didn't have our Bills. I can still remember we were all standing, holding hands when Scott attempted that kick."

Finally the moment arrived. Up in the ABC broadcast booth came the call from Al Michaels: "Norwood tries to kick his longest ever on grass. Forty-seven yards. Eight seconds left. Adam Lingner will snap it." Then, as the ball drifts wide of the right upright, "No good. Wide right."

"Some's been made of the hold," Reich acknowledged years later. "The one thing on a long field goal, you don't want the ball to be moving. So I get the snap, I put the ball down, and there's a split second where I don't see the laces. Like they were behind my face mask or something, and the laces were, as they say, out. They were faced away from me. So you've got a split second there where you can spin the laces to try and get them going directly forward, or they were a little away from me. So my decision, my decision before the snap was I wanna give him a clean look without the ball spinning because Scott tended to have a pretty quick tempo. You just don't want him to kick the laces. The laces were kinda pointed at me a little bit, then I decided. I basically suppose I decided to let it go, give him a clean look at it."

Were the laces right?

"That's not something I even delve into," Norwood said in an interview with ESPN years later. "The ball, wherever it's sitting down, that's what I take. In this instance, however, the laces were [out]. I didn't feel like it was a contributing factor. It's all part of it. It's definitely a team situation."

Reich still wonders about the most famous play in the history of the Buffalo Bills. He had placed the laces to the right—the direction in which the ball tailed off. Would it have made a difference if he had positioned the ball differently for Norwood?

"We'll never know. In theory, some people would say if the laces are," and here Reich's voice trails off like the kick, "I don't think so. Let's put it this way: you'd like to get the perfect snap and the perfect hold. And what I would say is it was a good snap and a good hold, but it wasn't perfect. We made a lot of kicks like that. Let's just put it that way."

Pete Metzelaars was blocking on the play. "I was on the left wing and I blocked and spun around and watched the kick," he remembered. "It was hooking, and all of a sudden, a gust of wind came up and it just straightened out a little bit. The first instinct was, you could see it hooking in. You're like, *It's going in.*"

Reich will never forget the sound of that kick: "What I remember is he kicked it so hard and so pure he kind of grunted when he kicked it, which he would do every now and then when he was kicking a longer kick, and he gave this grunt. Here's one of my takes on it, and I don't know whether it's right, wrong, or indifferent: you know sometimes in golf you think you've hit a putt too hard it goes through the break. And whether it was fate or something, rather than the ball hooking in, the ball actually at the last 20 yards kind of veered to the right a little bit. And it's not the only time I've seen that happen, but it's just very rare.

"I saw the flight of the ball the whole way. I got a great view. About three-quarters of the way there, I thought it was gonna be in. The thing is, it's a 47-yard field goal and it goes by the upright about three-quarters of the way up. I'm telling you that thing would have been 65 yards. My theory is, he hit it so pure that rather than the ball taking its natural little hook in, and I don't know if it was a breeze, but the ball hooks out to the right a little bit. The only time I've ever seen that happen is two times out of every 100 kicks."

From where Polian was standing, he was certain the kick was true. "The ball was snapped and up it went, and I said, 'We're world champions! We're world champions!' And it just went right at the last minute."

Kelso was standing on the sideline holding his teammates' hands. "I just recall not looking. I didn't look. I couldn't. I just waited for the reaction. I could see Marv. I could see a couple of our other guys and across the way to the Giants sideline. And I saw Marv just put his head down, and their guys jumping up and down, so I knew it was not a good result. It was tough. It was tough."

The kick had the distance, just not the necessary accuracy required to make Buffalo the world champion. When the ball drifted wide to the outside of the right goal post, it delivered a second Super Bowl title in five years to the Giants.

Norwood, and all the Bills, looked lost. With his right hand, the kicker briefly rubbed his eyes as he made his way back toward the bench. Several teammates patted him on the shoulder or gave him a quick hug.

"It was out of his range," Polian says now, more than 20 years later. "He was almost perfect from about 44 in, so it was just outside his range. But nonetheless, he gave it a great shot, and it just veered wide right. And that was it, the ballgame."

"I can't speak for Scott," Reich said, "but based on pregame, I would have aimed for the right upright and figure it's gonna hook in a little bit. And that ball, when it was kicked, was going right at the right upright and most times it's gonna come in and it just veered out to the right, which is highly unusual. But I don't think the ball started outside the upright. I think it was right at the upright and at the last second veers to the right."

As the ball sailed off course, not one of his teammates could believe what they were witnessing. "Oh no," Metzelaars thought. "It just faded out to the right. I remember talking afterward with Frank Reich. He'd been hooking all those kicks in all through warm-ups and stuff, so he played the hook, and all of a sudden, just a little bit of wind came up, and all of a sudden, it just straightened up and it went a few feet off to the right."

"I just remember watching the ball go up, and from my angle it looked like it went through," Darryl Talley said. "But it went right."

From where he was standing on the sidelines, Bill Parcells couldn't tell where the kick was going. "I thought he hit it pretty good, but I couldn't tell where it was at all. Really when I knew was when our players started jumping. You know that was before the kick finished. Some of them, you know, they know that he missed it. So I see that and, of course, that's when the players were jumping, lifting me on top of them. They do all that."

Even to this day, Polian will say, "It was tough. The terrible feeling of loss was tempered by the fact we knew we played a darn good football team. And when you come within an inch of winning the world championship, you've got nothing to be ashamed about or nothing to hang your head over. And that was the message that Marv and the rest of us preached to each other and to the players in the locker room: don't hang your heads. You've had a great season. It's a tough break. That's the way it goes. Let's come back strong."

Norwood did not hide in the trainer's room or hang his head in defeat. He simply stood in front of his locker to face the media—albeit somewhat dazed, a man lost in a boy's game—and began to answer their questions politely and patiently. "You get one shot," he said. "You do the best you can. It's never a guarantee from that distance, never a chip shot. I hit it good, but maybe I didn't swivel my hips enough on it and follow through as much as I would have liked. I may have tried to get too much leg into it."

When he appeared with Lynn Swann near the end of ABC's television coverage of the Super Bowl, he was asked what he had been thinking on that final drive. "I was excited about the opportunity," Norwood began, "kept saying to myself, 'Jim, get it down there. I want to kick this one for the team.' Just a situation where you get one opportunity. It obviously didn't work out. I knew it was a long kick and I may have emphasized too much trying to get a lot of leg into it. May have taken away from the follow through a bit and…you don't get a second opportunity. If I had a second opportunity, I might do something a little bit different."

Then he took a slight pause and continued in an almost stream-of-conscious way. "I missed an opportunity for this football team. I feel badly. I let a lot of people down. You realize in this profession you have to come back off times like this. I'm certain I'll do that."

He may not have been carried off the field that night, but he carried himself like a man.

Later he would tell *Sports Illustrated,* "Early on in the kick, you have your head down, you're kicking it. About two-thirds of the way there, I could pretty much tell it was going to be wide. I had prepared as well as I could. I had done the best I could. The biggest thing about that kick was not how it impacted me, but how it let the team down. I could look myself in the mirror."

They had come so far, through some god-awful seasons when they could hardly ever win as well as seasons that ended with painful defeats in the playoffs.

And now this.

Never *anything* like this.

In a frenzy they had just moved down the field against a tremendous Giants defense and were so close to finishing the most important comeback any of them would ever know.

This close.

"Heartache," Kelly called it. "All the hard work we put in. All the people, my family, my mom and dad, and all my brothers who had supported me all the way through high school and college and my NFL career, I felt for them and the city of Buffalo, all our great fans."

Up in the stands on the 40-yard line, Dennis DiPaolo was celebrating. "It looked like he made it. We're all cheering and jumping up and down until we looked across the field, and our guys were like, *What the heck?* It looked like he had made it. And we were like you have to be kidding," he remembered.

"We all squeezed and used body language and we all groaned and it was wide right," Ange Coniglio recalls.

At his frat house, Bob Coniglio said, "A lot of us didn't think Norwood had the leg strength. I remember when we made it down to about the 30 we were saying, 'It's going to be close.' We didn't think he was going to kick it far enough. There were always people going, 'He doesn't have a strong enough leg.' But when he got out there, we all thought he was going to make the kick.

"One room went ballistic, and the other room pretty much went dead silent. We can't believe we just saw that. There was a snowstorm outside in Buffalo, and we walked a couple of blocks from our fraternity house to our other house and we saw a couple of Bills fans just standing there, shaking their heads. I can't believe he missed that kick."

Peter Nussbaum was a college student in Buffalo who remembers that first Super Bowl as "a day as vivid for me as any from college. The fraternity house was completely divided. I remember the kick and I remember walking out of the house that was on Heath Street, right near the south campus. Everyone just walking up that street with their heads hung low. It was a terribly deflating moment. But it was well worth it."

As he followed the flight of the ball and realized the game was gone, Kelly leaned to his right to get a better look, then turned around, away from the field, and took off his helmet. For a moment it looked as if he might throw it to the ground while all along the sideline his teammates cursed and hung their heads and kicked the ground.

Across the field the Giants were celebrating wildly, jumping up and down and hugging each other, as their quarterback, Jeff Hostetler, was getting ready to take one final snap and kneel down to end the closest Super Bowl game ever played. The Giants hoisted Parcells up in the air and began to carry him off the field. But the winning coach was searching for his counterpart in all the mayhem. "I was looking for Marv," Parcells said. "I wanted desperately to see him, but I couldn't get down to shake his hand. So I just had to kind of salute him. A salute, and I knew he understood that."

The euphoria carried into the Giants locker room, where Parcells was trumpeting what may have been the greatest victory of his career, saying, "Winning is better than sex." Laughing at the memory of this years later, he tried to put that in a better context. "You know, you say some things you wished you hadn't said. I was trying to describe the euphoria that goes along with winning the championship. Whether you've won it before or not, you know it's a special, special feeling that bonds everybody in the room together."

Immediately after winning his first Super Bowl four years earlier, Parcells had told his team when they reached the locker room
before the television cameras and the media poured in, "They can
never take this away from you." Now, more than a quarter of a
century later, that still rings true. "It's the truth," the coach said.
"Because just for a short moment, but it's fleeting, you're on top of
your profession, on top of your industry. You're on top, and very
few people get to say that. They just can't take that away from you.
They can say, 'Hey, you were this, you were that, you weren't any
good.' Well, you know what? You've always got that trophy to show
'em. It's nice."

The years go by, but the championship seasons endure. Not
long ago the Giants' first Super Bowl championship team celebrated
its 25th anniversary. "I've been to some reunions now, and those are
very special things," Parcells said. "And it's not much different than
it used to be. And we went to a reunion last year, our '86 championship team, and all but two players were there. One was taking his
son to visit a college, and the other was in Africa on a safari...And
seeing those guys, it's...25 years later, but it's like time doesn't..."
His voice trails off, caught in a moment from the past.

The game can break your heart or lift your spirit. The pain
of defeat trumps the joy of victory on every given Sunday. When
fortune smiles on you, it is fleeting at best. So you better find joy
in the quest, beauty in the pursuit, fulfillment in the seemingly little inconsequential moments that can provide a smile years later.
For the Giants coach, such a moment occurred more than an hour
before kickoff in Tampa.

Walking around the field watching his players stretching and
going through various drills, Parcells noticed someone he thought
he knew at the far end of the field down by the Buffalo end zone.

It was a priest, Father John Manion, who had served the Bills on gamedays since Chuck Knox coached the team back in the 1970s. Knox had known Father Manion from the time he was an assistant with the New York Jets during the mid-1960s in the AFL.

Parcells knew Father Manion when the priest was at Seton Hall in northern New Jersey, and the coach would help the university in various ways. "Boy, you know I did a lot of work and fund-raisers for Seton Hall," Parcells recalls, "and tried to help their program. And I was friends with Father Manion, and we knew each other well. I'd see him at lunch at this restaurant, Manny's, near Giants Stadium I used to go to. He used to go there. So, this is really funny. We're out there in warm-ups, and he's got his Bills jacket on and he's down the other end and doesn't want me to see him or see me. And he really doesn't want this encounter. But I'm looking, staring him down, way down there in warm-ups. He's about 30, 40 yards from me. He's got this Bills jacket on, you know one of those satin ones. And so he finally gives me a kind of short little wave, and I kinda take my fingers across my chest like from the letters 'Bills' across the jacket and then I sort of open my palms like, you know, 'What's this?'

"He just kind of gives me a push away with his hand from 30 yards. He doesn't want to see it or hear it or talk about it, okay? So now the game's over, and I'm sitting on the team bus getting ready to go back to the hotel there in Tampa, and here comes Father Manion and he's got a Giants jacket on. He's gotta find a Giants jacket and stand right there in the window of the bus and show me that he's got a Giants jacket on."

All these years later, the coach still laughs about it, saying, "He didn't want to talk to me in warm-ups."

Now looking back on that game across a lifetime spent in football, coaching at the highest level and reaching the greatest pinnacle of the game, that day in Tampa may well have been the most gratifying Parcells ever spent on a football field. "I don't think anybody on that field, until that last unfortunate-for-them kick, good for us...really knew anything about what the eventual outcome was going to be because it was a hard fought game, a classic game, played by pretty good teams," Parcells said. "I've always said this and I really believe this and I'm speaking in a very prejudicial way because I was the coach of the Giants. I thought had we lost that game it would have been a shame. I really felt like we outplayed them—you know, when you look at the whole 60 minutes. But that being said, they still had a chance to win. It was just good fortune for us it just didn't happen."

It all came down to the final seconds. The Bills came up a little wide and one point short. Their pain was palpable. "Everybody was mad," Talley said. "And everybody started blaming Scotty. But we all had chances to make plays that would have made a difference and Scotty had won other games for us."

Talley looked at Cornelius Bennett, and as they began to leave the field he could only say, "Fuck, we just lost this. Fuck, we let this one get away."

The magnitude of the defeat almost immediately began to gnaw at Talley. "We'll keep our heads up, we'll be back," he kept telling himself. "We lost this one. We let this one get away. Fuck, we'll be back."

In the quiet of the Bills locker room, Levy addressed his team. The coach could barely bring himself to talk. Choking back emotion he looked around the room and said, "There isn't a loser in this room." There were no war references from this student of history.

No lyrical passages from this white-haired gentleman who held a master's degree in literature from Harvard. No inspiring clarion call to the future. It was as if his mind was frozen in time, back out there on the field. Eight seconds left. The ball drifting wide right. His head bowed down in defeat.

He also would not utter a word about next year. "I would address that at a later time," Levy said, the anguish of those moments forever burnished in his mind. "I didn't want to give a long speech. As a coach you have to say something, and I wanted them to know how proud I was of them. How proud I was of the valiant way they fought."

He scanned the room and made his way to Norwood's locker. "I was trying to think what to say to him, and I couldn't find the words," Levy recalled. Then, as the coach sat silently next to his somber kicker, a couple of players made it a point to stop by and console their teammate. "I sat there next to Scott," Levy said, "and Darryl Talley came up to him and said, 'If we'd made that tackle on that last touchdown drive, it wouldn't have come down to that.' Andre Reed said, 'If I would have hung on to that pass on the 15-yard line in the first half, it would have been a touchdown.' And on and on. And they all took responsibility."

Many years later, after he was out of football and had replayed that kick over and over again in his mind, Norwood came to understand, "That's the thing about our past. You can't make it any better, you can't make it any worse. You can't do anything to change it."

The game had been televised by ABC Sports, which afforded the network's Buffalo television affiliate immediate access to the Bills' locker room upon its conclusion. Bob Koshinski was the first television reporter to go live and he promptly interviewed Norwood, Kelly, Steve Tasker, and Talley. Koshinski remembered, "As I was doing some of the toughest interviews I've ever done as a sports reporter, I remember thinking, 'Gee, they came so close. They may never get back.' The Bills offense just couldn't get on the field. They only had the ball for 19 minutes and scored a point a minute. It took them this long to get here. They may never get back."

When the team returned home the very next afternoon, the good people of Buffalo held a celebration at Niagara Square in the center of town. The crowd was estimated to be between 25,000 to 30,000 fans. Everywhere you looked there were still Super Bowl signs hanging from street signs and office buildings, cars bearing decorations and Bills insignias, store windows and billboards, and even rooftops all covered with reminders of Super Bowl week. In the days leading up to the game, the town had come alive. "For the people of Buffalo, the Buffalo Bills was something to look forward to, it keeps you going," Koshinski said. "You talk about the game on Monday and every day as you get closer to the next game on Sunday. It's just a way of life. And you just knew they'd never stop talking about this one."

In a way the fans assembled were already looking forward to next season while cheering wildly one last time for the season that had just brought them so much joy. They were hardworking people, these men and women of the Rust Belt who found such joy and refuge in this team that somehow managed to relieve the stress of the hard times that had hit their city. "It was really upbeat," Nussbaum remembered of the scene all these years later. "There was a ton of pride. It was a relatively small city and it was on the national stage, and there was a tremendous amount of pride associated with the Bills."

And the fans were loyal—never more so than now, when the members of their extended family were hurting. "That's what a Bills fan is," said one fan, who grew up around Buffalo and attended many games. "That's where we get our strength. That you're not in it alone. You've got people hugging and high-fiving. It was just something extraordinary."

Donn Bartz left work early that day to be there for the rally on the steps of City Hall. "Everybody was afraid when Scotty Norwood would come out that people would boo him, but they didn't," he said. "The game was over, and you still love your players, and that's all that counted. You're not gonna knock us down. We're there. We're fans. You're our players. What're you gonna do? We're gonna stand by 'em. Like when Kelly came in and arrived in town. If you could get out of work, you were down there. It's a feeling you get inside, *I gotta be there,* and you go. You might be five blocks away from the action, but at least you can say 'I was there.' They had speakers set up, so you didn't have any problem hearing."

There was really only one player they wanted to hear from that day. The only one they wanted to speak up. He was the one man they wanted to lift up. Only he had a hard time getting out the words he wanted to share with them. He could barely speak and shook his head and rubbed his eyes. Many years later, when he made an infrequent trip to Buffalo, Scott Norwood said, "Their reaction was not to attack in any way but to embrace and support me, and that's what I felt in the air. I had tried my best to express that back to them. It's something I'll always carry with me."

And so it was on that winter afternoon in January 1991, when they all began to reach out to him, their chant rising: "We love Scott! We love Scott! We love Scott."

In practically no time at all, just a couple of seconds, their plea started to build to a crescendo and echo throughout the downtown square, filling up the heart of Buffalo.

CHAPTER 5 | The Pride of Buffalo

WHEN THE American Football League announced in 1959 that Buffalo would to field one of its eight teams, it seemed to lift the spirit of upstate New York. Those truly were the good old days for this working-class American city. Big industries seem to stretch out in every direction: Bethlehem Steel, Republic Steel, Anaconda, General Motors, Ford, and Dunlop, companies that enriched the American dream and experience, thrived in and around Buffalo. With the advent of a professional football team, Buffalo had finally achieved major-league status. Everyone, it seemed, was enthusiastic and bursting with civic pride. It hardly mattered that the Bills would be playing in creaky old Buffalo War Memorial Stadium—"the old rock pile," as it was dismissively known—which was often used for stock car races.

"It was just a great time and it was a different time," Donn Bartz, one of the first season-ticket holders said. "We used to be able to bring in our lunches, cases of beer, and you'd sit there and eat and drink and enjoy the game."

Tailgate parties right on the 50-yard line. How much better can it get?

The city of Buffalo may have gained a professional football team, but it never lost its small-town aura. "We'd park right on the streets or in somebody's front yard. Not like nowadays," Bartz said. Those really were the golden days before personal seat licenses, corporate suites, and preferred parking fees began to fleece fans.

By 1970, when the Bills and the rest of the AFL merged into the NFL, plans were already under way to build a new stadium in Buffalo, one befitting a team that had won two AFL championships. "The merger really gave pride to the city," Bartz said. "We really felt the pride of saying 'we belong to the NFL.' It gave some credence to the city. We were a major-league town."

One developer even wanted to build an all-weather stadium—*a dome!*—in suburban Lancaster, but the local high school protested, and that proposal was eventually dropped. At that time the city was experiencing economic stress. Buffalo's aging steel industry and obsolete processes were no longer profitable, and Bethlehem Steel practically shuttered its entire operation. Other industries were departing for the Sun Belt. In the two decades from 1960 to 1980, nearly 40,000 factory jobs were lost. The fragmentation brought about by urban renewal exacted a terrible price: large pockets of neighborhoods were razed and citizens were moved into high-rise projects. The ethnic and diverse middle class was all but uprooted; communities—built upon immigration and migration and supported by work in the steel and manufacturing industries with substantial union wages—suffered.

Finally, after years of litigation, a new 80,000-seat stadium was erected on the outskirts of Buffalo, in Orchard Park, under the management of Frank Schoenle and his construction company. By the time the new venue opened for business in 1973, it had already been named Rich Stadium after a local corporation, Rich Products—for a fee. Ralph Wilson had negotiated a 25-year, $1.5 million deal for the stadium's naming rights, one of the earliest such marketing agreements in American sports. Wilson was even canny enough to work out a compromise with the company who wanted the stadium to be named Coffee Rich Stadium after its premier product. A quarter of a century later, when the agreement expired, the stadium was renamed Ralph Wilson Stadium—but only after the Rich Corporation balked at paying a whopping new rights fee, which would have brought the price up to par with other naming rights at the time.

For all but a few months of the year, the Bills were the lifeblood of the town. From the time in midsummer when they reported to training camp until well after the last game of the season, in virtually every town in upstate New York fans devoured football tidbits and gossiped about their team. Long before sports talk radio, the Bills commanded 24/7 coverage throughout the region.

"When football came it gave a release to the people, so they had something besides work in their lives," Bartz said, "something else to occupy their time and make them feel good. It wasn't just work, eat, and sleep. You have your coffee break at the water cooler and you're always talking about the team. A lot of people would talk until Wednesday or maybe even Thursday about how bad we were last Sunday. If it was a tough loss, you didn't start looking ahead to the next game until Friday. Some people, it eats at them for quite a while. I have a few friends like that. But that's the nature of the beast. We live and die football. We live and die Bills."

Bill Polian believes the bond between the team and the town is "unique, to use a euphemism." He said of that passion, "It only exists in Green Bay—and Boston with baseball—in professional sports. Yeah it's regional, but it's 365 days of the year, 24 hours of the day. The thing that's unique about Buffalo is that in most other cities it will be the business leaders who tend to be transplants. That's just the nature of business in America. Politicians and people who work in government, they may be casual fans they're not real hard-core fans. But Buffalo's different.

"The congressman who represented the south towns where the stadium is located, and where the vast majority of us live, was Jack Kemp, a former Bills quarterback. The county executive was Ed Rutkowski, a former Bill. The mayor when I was there was Jimmy Griffin, a legendary guy who was loved for his down to earth, everyman qualities and was a brilliant politician and mayor as well."

Griffin is best remembered for his outspoken ways. During the blizzard of 1985, he suggested the people in Buffalo should "go home, buy a six-pack of beer, and watch a good football game." He was forever known as "Jimmy Six-Pack."

These men, who ran the city, shared at least one thing in common with each and every one of their constituents: they cared passionately about their Bills. Several of them would gather at the Quarterback Club every Monday after a home game during the football season in a restaurant in Memorial Auditorium where the politicians would flank Polian on the dais. "You had up to 1,500 people there," Polian said, "and lunch was being served and the mayor would say to me, 'Hey Bill, what are we going to do about right corner? We got to get play out of right corner. We're getting picked on. What are we going to do about this?'" Polian laughs, as if he still has to answer for that a quarter of a century later. "But he was a dyed-in-the-wool fan. I mean he cared about the Bills as much as he cared about anything else. And that's the way it was,

365 days of the year, 24 hours a day. Everything Bills, all the time. People really cared."

It was a birthright to be a Bills fan, as if your parents had signed some certificate at the hospital before they brought you home, a baptismal right. "Most importantly, every young child who comes into the world in western New York for the 10 years I was there was born a Bills fan," Polian said. "They were brought into a Bills family and he or she was a Bills fan from Day One."

Of course, the fans had not always reacted with such a religious fervor. When Polian arrived, attendance was at an all-time low, and there was talk of the Bills relocating to places such as Seattle or Jacksonville. Polian knew one of his foremost challenges was to build a strong and loyal fan base. If you build that, the players will come.

"We needed to try and create new ways to try and sell the team in the marketplace," Polian said. "We felt we needed some corporate support, and some corporate leaders were great along those lines. And the biggest outfit to come out of that effort was Marine Midland Bank, and we hit the nail on the head. We made retail tickets available through the bank outlets. We created the Shout Zone, the signature for that campaign. We didn't discount tickets, but we kept pricing realistic for the marketplace. We played one preseason game at home instead of two, which effectively created a discount. We discounted season tickets as opposed to individual over-the-counter gameday sales. And that combination, coupled with extensive availability in the branches in western New York, made it really a good thing. We started to move tickets and started some esprit de corps, teamwork with bank employees, and got it going in the right direction."

As Polian began to construct a better team, attendance began to steadily increase. It wasn't as if the Bills were in the fight of their lives for the entertainment dollar in western New York. They were pretty much the only game in the region. Sure Buffalo had a philharmonic and a first-rate art museum, but football—well, that was the big show. The Bills gave citizens a different sense of self-esteem. It gave them a national identity.

Dick Zolnowski, who was a police officer in Buffalo for 21 years, remembers the surge in pride he felt when the Bills advanced to the 1988 AFC Championship Game. "On every street corner they were selling Bills souvenirs and they had lines down the streets," he said. "You'd go to other cities, and when they heard I was from Buffalo, they were really excited, and all they wanted to hear was stories about Kelly and Thomas and Bennett. I was in Fort Lauderdale to see my brother, and it was around Christmastime. People wanted to know what were the players really like, what was going on in Buffalo. It made me feel really good. I was like the hit of the party. Buffalo, you would think it was New York City or London. You were from Buffalo. You were at the top."

Well, maybe not New York or London. But the Bills certainly put Buffalo on the map. The old cop laughs at the memory of it now. And he still remembers the kindness the players would grant to strangers. One day Zolnowski came upon James Lofton in a mall, "and he would stop and talk with you. I don't know anybody who was ever turned away by one of the Bills in those days. The players were really nice. They were kind. They were so popular, and people were so behind them."

One fan, who grew up in Allegeny, New York, not far from Buffalo, thinks it's all part of everyone's DNA. "It's just a weird dynamic," he says. "It's kind of a depressed part of the country.

But when the Bills do well, everybody does well. It's just a very tight-knit kind of fabric. You feel like, 'this is my team, and we're up against the big boys.' When they do well, it's just phenomenal. The next day at work, the day after, everybody's happy. 'Oh, did you see that game? Can you believe that play?' So it's more of psyche. Other cities may be passionate about their teams, but it's not part of their psyche."

Ange Coniglio, a retired engineer who worked and taught in Buffalo and has lived there his whole life, is convinced "every Buffalonian probably has an inferiority complex about Buffalo, where it sits in the pantheon of big cities around the country. I'm a Buffalonian. I love it. I can't explain it. It's unbelievably diverse in its culture. You can do almost anything you want to do in Buffalo. If you're an outdoorsman, there's hunting and fishing very close by. My family has a cottage in nearby Crystal Beach, Ontario, which is 30 minutes away from my house here on Lake Erie. It's crystal clear. It's not rotten or spoiled, which is why the name of the beach is Crystal Beach. So there's a lot about Buffalo that outsiders don't know or recognize. But it's not a big city. It's a small city. I've never been in a traffic jam in Buffalo."

Except maybe on gameday. Cars begin lining up outside the parking lots before they opened at 8:00 in the morning, and those who have recreational vehicles would get together in the RV lot and make it a weekend excursion, driving in on Saturday and driving out on Monday morning. No matter how cold it got, they would set up portable barbecue grills and picnic tables and lawn chairs, as if they were vacationing at the beach. "We'd set up little community dinners with six or eight RV units," Don Pitts said. It was a "community atmosphere. You get to meet a lot of people."

"The great thing about tailgating up there is you could be poor and hungry and walk from one car to the next and you would be fed and taken care of," the Allegeny fan said. "It doesn't matter who you are, what the color of your skin is. It's come on here, have a dog, have a kielbasa, have a burger. And that's really cool. You could just walk up to another tailgate and start talking and everyone's kind of like a big family. Camaraderie was big."

"Buffalos' a pretty friendly place," Coniglio said. "[The Bills] made their relationships stronger. I wouldn't say it just brought them together, but it made them stronger. It's too bad it took a football team to do that, that people couldn't do that without sports, but it certainly helped. Everyone had an opinion on the Bills—grandmothers, students in grammar schools."

You could walk up to a stranger on those frigid days and all you had to do was mention the Bills to break the ice. "All you had to say was, 'How about that last touchdown? Or that last touchdown Andre scored? And they knew what you were talking about," Coniglio continued. "Buffalonians are close to begin with, but it brought them closer together."

"Buffalo is known as the City of Good Neighbors," Polian said, "and it's because of the weather conditions and the harsh winters, and people have to band together and help each other. It's just the nature of things and it's an ethos that exists in the city and in the region. And, as a result, when you're with the Buffalo Bills you're part of the community. Yeah, they're heroes and they're stars, but they're your friends and neighbors, too."

Mark Kelso said, "You would pull up to a traffic light and the guy in the car next to you would be waving at you, wishing you good luck in your next game. It was like a small town, and everybody knew who you were and they were all behind you in every game. That's why we always felt nobody could beat us at home."

Jim Kelly has never forgotten how much those fans meant to their team. "That's why, during my era, we had the 12th Man up on our Wall of Fame," the Hall of Fame quarterback said. "That to us was a part of the reason we were so successful because we knew how important that 12th Man was. Before I got there the team wasn't doing very well. The record was bad. Everything was down, even the economy. Steel mills closed down, and people were losing their jobs. And when we started winning, it brought the city back to life and everybody got excited."

The fans didn't just root for their Bills. They believed they could relate to them. From the day Kelly joined the Bills, he gave them all a reason to believe. Kelso remembered the atmosphere around training camp when the quarterback arrived. "Camp was really open, and anyone who wanted to come could come," he said. "And 95 percent of the time we'd have a couple of hundred people there. And the day Jim showed up, we had 5,000 people there. And you could see he was their kind of guy, the piece we were missing to get to the next level. It's a blue-collar community of hardworking people, and Jim kind of epitomized that. He'd give you the shirt off his back."

It was as if the fans and players gave each other life support. And the players didn't just show up for their fans on Sunday afternoons. During the week and especially in the offseason, they could be counted on to give back to the community. Zolnowski recalled, "A lot of the players used to volunteer for Meals on Wheels, where you feed people; City Mission; Friends of the Night, where the homeless people would come in. Cornelius Bennett was one of them, Thurman was doing it. Pete Metzelaars had 65 Roses for MS, multiple sclerosis. That was his big charity."

It seemed everyone was on the Bills bandwagon. Everyone had a stake in the team, an investment in their city.

"You'd go see your kids' school events, and people would say, 'How's Thurman? Everything all right?'" Polian said. "And they'd begin a knowledgeable conversation about the team or they'd talk about how our own kids were playing. It was an everyday existence, and you're part of it. You work there and you're a highly public person, and people get very excited and very invested in it. I'll put it this way: there wasn't a lot of extraneous hero worship and not a lot of resentment, which today exists, and certainly not red-carpet celebrity as we know it."

Which isn't to say the players didn't receive royal treatment. The Empire Sports Network had four Buffalo Bills television programs running each week: *The Thurman Thomas Show, The Frank Reich Show, The Don Beebe Show,* and *The Bill Polian Show.* "Back in those days whenever you turned on the TV set, you could never miss seeing those shows says Zolnowski, who's had season tickets since 1969. "Everybody had their own show on different stations. You could get in there and ask questions of the players. At that time Kelly owned a restaurant called Sports City Grill right downtown and every Wednesday he would tape the show. You could have a nice dinner and stay for the show. Every time you'd go in there, you'd run into Pete Metzelaars or Cornelius Bennett.

"Most of them were nice, most of them were kind to the fans. I remember one particular time Cornelius was at a table, and a bunch of kids came over to him wanting his autograph. He was there with his lady friend and he said, 'I'm eating. After we're done come on over, and I'll give you all the autographs you want.' And you could understand that. He was very polite. He didn't want to hurt the kids' feelings. And he gave them all the autographs they wanted."

The fans reveled in their team's good fortune because it had been such a long time coming. Bartz is an accountant who worked for a buttoned-down company. During one losing streak years ago in an effort to bring the team some luck, he decided he wasn't going to shave until the Bills finally won a game.

So one Monday morning upon entering the elevator his boss nudged him, "Don't you think you should shave when you come to work?" Bartz explained that he would—when the Bills won. His boss understood, "All right. I'll go along with that."

The city dressed up or, rather, dressed down for their team every week. Casual Fridays set the tone. Everybody was caught up in the spirit of the town. Everyone wore the uniform of the day. "The people in the business community would do dress down Fridays, which meant you didn't have to wear suits, you could wear Bills colors, Bills gear," Dennis DiPaolo said. "On a Friday everyone was wearing Buffalo Bills T-shirts, jerseys, everything. My cousin Aldo was running a beautiful men's store for suits. Thank God he had the Bills coming into his store. But that's the way the whole city was. It was just electric."

"It didn't get any better than football weekends," Dennis said. "We were on national TV, and Chris Berman was coming into town for dinner and he'd have veal parmigiana my father would prepare. And the players were going into my cousin Aldo's shop almost on a weekly basis because we knew the media was all going to be here, and they wanted to look their best."

Sunday nights, just before midnight, *George Michael's Sports Machine,* a nationally syndicated highlight show would come on. "Back in those days there was pretty much only local sports on TV," Coniglio remembers from his college years. "George Michael's show was a big deal, and Monday morning I'd drive over to the gas station to get *The Buffalo News.* I'd stand there in the lot and read the paper. You couldn't get enough about the game."

Don Pitts was a sales rep with Altria and he would spend the week driving around western New York for work, listening to WGR 55, a talk radio station that was consumed with football during the season. "You hated to miss it," he said, "because you might miss out on something. It was pretty much constant talk about the Bills."

Everywhere throughout upstate New York where Pitts' work took him, his business associates all wanted to hear about the Bills. "If we had a meeting in Syracuse, three hours away, they knew my appreciation for the Bills and what a fan I was," he says, "and they would wear a Bills collared shirt to my meetings and always make comments about them to show their support. People realized the Bills were special."

All those Buffalo fans waited a long time before they finally got to see a home playoff game. It was New Year's Day 1989, and only 80,000 were fortunate enough to make their way into Rich Stadium when the Bills defeated the Houston Oilers 17–10, to mark the start of a new era. By then the Bills were on their way to becoming a Super Bowl team, and their fans were a strong factor in their success. "You'd go out on the field, and there are fans you literally end up developing a personal relationship with—a unique bond." Frank Reich said. "You go out on the field and you're warming up and you acknowledge certain people. There was a group of guys who sat over behind the visitors' bench, and every time you'd go out on the field you'd acknowledge those guys. After games you'd talk to them a little bit. I think there was a closer bond between the players and the fans. It comes in degrees. There's a connection to the fans, a connection to the city that other teams in other cities don't have. It's just that in those years the degree, the level of it was very high." All these years later Reich smiles. "I still get phone calls and email from some of them."

To Coniglio, Bills games were something akin to High Mass. "My wife and I are true, avid fans," he said. "If the phone rings between 1:00 and 4:00 on Sunday, we don't answer it. We watch the game all by ourselves or with very close family. The first Super Bowl, we made the mistake of going out to a party. It was a great party until that final kick. That was devastating. We went with old friends and we were enjoying ourselves, but when that kick didn't go through, that was it. I don't know if we even said good-bye that night. Everybody just walked home and cried in their beer."

Even with the bitter taste of that defeat, Coniglio managed to find a silver lining in those dark clouds overhead. "I have kids who always played a lot of sports and I always told my kids you learn a lot more from losing than you do from winning. And that's true. That doesn't mean I like it."

Clearly the fans were becoming as resilient and resourceful as their Bills. In the summer following the dispiriting loss to the New York Giants, one of them who had traveled to Tampa began to make plans for the very next Super Bowl game in Minneapolis. "People laughed at me," Zolnowski recalled. "In August, right in the middle of the preseason games, I reserved seven rooms in Minneapolis. My daughter had a part-time job with one of the hotel chains, the Holiday Inn. So the hotel called me back because they thought there was a mistake on my part and they charge extra for the Super Bowl week. People started to laugh at me because I got my hotel rooms in August.

"Well, come December, people were coming up to my seat on the 40-yard line and saying, 'You got any more rooms? You got any more rooms left?' I could've made a killing on that, but I didn't. I had the rooms under my name. We took two of them for my sister and her friend and my son and me. And the rest of them I had on standby. I did that every year. I had enough confidence the Bills were going to make it to the Super Bowl. And sure enough, it worked out."

CHAPTER 6 | Bouncing Back from Heartbreak

ALTHOUGH A LOSS on any given Sunday is always difficult to accept, no matter how narrow that defeat, the challenge of the next week's game quickly enhances a player's disposition and stimulates him to move forward.

But when you don't win the championship game, as is the case for all but one team in the NFL every year, the sense of frustration and even despair can haunt you for weeks, months, even a lifetime. "Football is different," Darryl Talley says. "You get one shot. In basketball they play seven games. Baseball, they play seven. We only get one shot."

One game for all time. Winner take all. The ball sails just wide of the goal post. Defeat kicks you in the face. Forever.

To this day Bill Polian still has difficulty getting over the anguish of that Super Bowl loss to the New York Giants. He is haunted by the fact that the Bills had run out of timeouts before they handed the ball to Thurman Thomas for their final offensive surge of the night. As soon as the ceremony at Niagara Square ended, Polian went straight to his office to watch the final sequence of the game. "I watched the tape and when I saw the draw break wide open, that was the most sickening feeling of all," he said years later, believing Thomas only needed to only get by Mark Collins for the game-winning touchdown. "Because, well, you can never, never say never, but I'm sure Thurman only had Collins to beat."

But, as replays confirmed, when Thurman began to cut back from the right sideline and toward an opening in the Giants defense, Collins managed to grab him up high, more than enough to slow him up and bring him down. "Ah," Polian said, "if Thurman had juked him, I think he goes all the way."

You think if he juked Collins he scores? "In my mind's eye," Polian maintained, "I can see him one-on-one, and I'll take Thurman in that matchup anytime."

Polian paused, still stung by the memory of it all. He was standing on the field that night, peering around players and coaches and officials to get a better look at the action. However, his mind has played games in the intervening years. Because as the play unfolded, Thurman did indeed turn away from the sideline and attempted to run to daylight, determined to get as many yards as he could. "All I remember is too bad we didn't have the timeout," Polian said, "because I think he would have probably juked him and gone all the way or at least gotten us down to the 10-yard line or something." Somewhere close enough that Norwood couldn't have missed.

Polian was hardly alone in his misery. Over and over again throughout another long, dreary winter in Buffalo, the fans could not stop talking about Norwood's missed kick. Everywhere the Bills went, it seemed all anyone wanted to talk about was how close they had come. It was never far from anyone's mind.

Don Pitts was just a fan, but no matter where his sales calls took him, he was always asked about the kick. That's how it was. As if it were in boldface headlines written all over him. THE KICK.

"No matter where you went, that was the big topic of conversation," he remembered. "You would relive the game all over again. You would talk about how it brought everybody to their feet. There were about 15 of us. We were all standing in the living room and holding hands. It was a pretty big letdown."

Jeff Wright, the nose tackle who had been in the middle of the trenches for so much of that night, remembers how difficult it was to put that game to rest. "Obviously it's a big letdown when you lose a Super Bowl," he said. "It's huge. It's hard to get over. It's incredibly hard. You replay all the plays that could have made a difference."

Scott Norwood's miss was only the final play that sealed Buffalo's fate. There had been other moments in the taut game that could have turned the game the Bills' way and, perhaps, altered the course of their history. Late in the opening quarter, the Bills offense began its only signature drive of the night, 12 plays that covered 80 yards with Kelly hitting Andre Reed four times for 44 yards. When Don Smith scored from the 1-yard line, the Bills took a 10–3 lead.

Although Buffalo failed to move the ball on its next three possessions, its lead increased to 12–3 in the second quarter when Giants quarterback Jeff Hostetler tripped over running back Ottis Anderson's right leg as the quarterback was retreating into the end zone to attempt a pass. Bruce Smith grabbed Hostetler by his right forearm and drove him hard to the ground, but somehow Hostetler managed to hold onto the ball. It was a safety, good for a nine-point advantage. Had Hostetler fumbled and Buffalo recovered, the Bills would have had a two-touchdown lead—a game changer.

Wright could not believe Hostetler held onto the ball. He could not believe it then. He cannot believe it now. "Four of us just piled on," Wright said. "Bruce Smith had his arm, Leon Seals and I were all over him, and he held on to the ball."

Would a touchdown there have changed the outcome? "I've thought that," Wright said. "But he made a great play. He held on to the ball."

"You know things happen that are game-affecting things that you just can't anticipate or expect to happen," Bill Parcells said of his quarterback's remarkable play. "My vantage point isn't very good when I'm down on the field there, so I don't know exactly what happened. But I've seen the footage now and, gee, that was closer than I thought it was. But I didn't know that when the ball-game was going on."

Darryl Talley was in on the play and he could not say that he was surprised to see Hostetler refuse to fumble. "I actually told everybody before the game, 'Look, Jeff's as tough as can be,'" Talley said, thinking back to his college days at West Virginia, when he first encountered Hostetler. "When Jeff was at Penn State and I knocked Todd Blackledge out of the game, Jeff came in and beat us. The game was at West Virginia. And the following year Jeff transferred to West Virginia. He was a tough, tough character who took his shots and then he'd get up and still throw the ball. And I told the guys beforehand he's strong as a bull, too. Don't be mistaken. Prime example: Bruce Smith had him in the end zone for a safety. He held onto the ball with one hand. This is Bruce Smith, 265 pounds, slamming you to the ground. Think about that. Think about that strength to hold himself up and hold onto that ball."

"That was a huge play," said Mark Kelso. "They were convinced they had to control the clock, and that's what they were able to do. That play allowed them stick to their game plan."

Joe Kelly, Jim's father (*top left*); Ilio DiPaolo (*top right*); Ilio's son, Dennis; (*bottom left*); and Jim Kelly wear matching Italian jackets. Ilio DiPaolo's was a popular Italian postgame hangout spot for the Bills. *(COURTESY DIPAOLO FAMILY)*

From left to right: Dennis DiPaolo, the son of a noted local restaurateur and wrestler; Bills linebacker Darryl Talley; and longtime Bills trainer Bud Carpenter pose together. *(COURTESY DIPAOLO FAMILY)*

Trading for linebacker Cornelius Bennett, the No. 2 overall pick in the 1987 NFL Draft, helped fortify the Bills defense.

Jim Kelly, who threw for 300 yards during the AFC Championship Game, steps back in the pocket during the Bills' 51–3 rout of the Raiders, which sent Buffalo to its first Super Bowl.

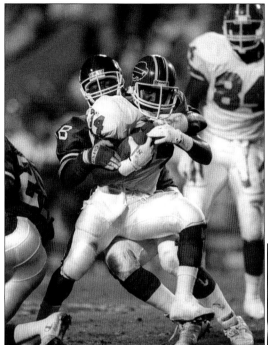

Giants linebacker Carl Banks tries to tackle Bills running back Thurman Thomas, who rushed for 135 yards on just 15 carries during Super Bowl XXV. *(GETTY IMAGES)*

Kicker Scott Norwood dejectedly walks off the field after missing a potential game-winning 47-yard field goal with eight seconds left in the 20–19 Super Bowl loss.

Steve Tasker's son, Deacon, helps console the special teams star after the Bills' 37–24 loss to the Redskins in Super Bowl XXVI.

Wide receiver Andre Reed (83) catches his third touchdown in the second half of Buffalo's 41–38 victory against the Oilers, which is the greatest postseason comeback in NFL history.

With his Cowboys already up 52–17 with less than five minutes in the fourth quarter of Super Bowl XXVII, defensive lineman Leon Lett showboats during his 65-yard fumble return. *(GETTY IMAGES)*

Symbolizing the persistence of the Buffalo Bills, wide receiver Don Beebe strips Leon Lett near the end zone after chasing down the defensive lineman who began celebrating too early. *(GETTY IMAGES)*

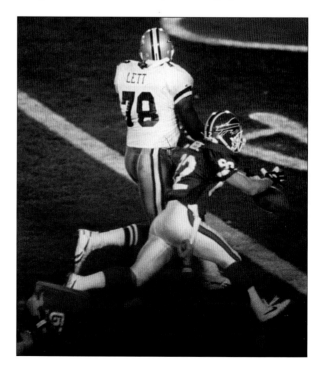

Defensive end Bruce Smith checks on Joe Montana after knocking out the Chiefs quarterback with a concussion during Buffalo's 30–13 victory in the AFC Championship Game. *(GETTY IMAGES)*

Because of the community's special bond with its team, Buffalo fans rejoice over the Bills' return to the Super Bowl—no matter what those on the national stage thought.

In the first minute of the second half of the Super Bowl rematch, safety James Washington returns a Thurman Thomas fumble 46 yards for a touchdown for the game-changing play of Super Bowl XXVIII. *(GETTY IMAGES)*

During his Pro Football Hall of Fame enshrinement in 2001, Marv Levy, whose steady hand guided the resilient Bills to four consecutive Super Bowls, stands next to his presenter, Bill Polian, the general manager who built those Bills teams. *(GETTY IMAGES)*

From left to right: Bruce Smith, Thurman Thomas, and Jim Kelly pose during Smith's Pro Football Hall of Fame enshrinement in 2009. Former Bills owner Ralph Wilson was also inducted that year.

With less than four minutes remaining in the first half, the Giants took over at their own 13-yard line and quickly moved down the field. When Hostetler connected on a key third-and-7 pass to Howard Cross for seven yards, the Giants were 14 yards from the Bills end zone with halftime quickly approaching. Cornelius Bennett batted down Hostetler's next pass with 39 seconds left, and the quarterback's second-down pass to Stephen Baker was too low. With one more stop, the Giants would have to settle for a field goal, and the Bills would hold a 12–6 lead at halftime. But on third down, Hostetler went right back to Baker, and this time he slipped past Nate Odomes on the end zone sideline for the Giants' first touchdown.

The Giants were revitalized heading to the locker room, and the Bills knew it. "We went in at halftime still up 12–10, but we felt like we had given a lot of stuff away," Metzelaars recalled. "We felt like we let them back in the game."

"That was big," Parcells said of Baker's touchdown, "because we were out there a long time, and they didn't get the ball very much. And then, of course, we started the third quarter with the same thing. A long drive—and going the same direction as a matter of fact."

The Giants opened the second half with a punishing, methodical 75-yard drive that culminated in a touchdown and gave them the lead 17–12. Four times on that drive the Giants faced third downs, and four times they converted. On their first third down, needing eight yards, Hostetler tossed a short pass to Dave Meggett, and the powerful 5'7" running back slithered through two Bills to complete an 11-yard gain. Three plays later on third-and-1, Ottis Anderson raced around left end for 24 yards.

Then the Bills defense seemed to right itself. But on third-and-13 Hostetler passed to Mark Ingram, who eluded the grasp of five Bills defenders before James Williams finally brought him down. As Ingram was tackled, he stretched out his arm, extending the ball for a first down, a pivotal play that covered 14 yards. Another Giants first down.

A few plays later, faced with a third-and-4, Hostetler bootlegged and arced a pass for nine yards to Howard Cross, putting the ball on the 3. Two plays after that, Anderson found the end zone.

Just five plays after Ingram had broken five tackles, the Giants had the upper hand—Ingram reaching for a vital first down, the play that sustained and defined the drive. The kind of play championship teams make.

"The Ingram Play," Talley practically spits the words out today. "I think that was one of the biggest plays in the game. A crucial play. I went for him up high and nearly took his head off, but I didn't make the play. He didn't go down. I chased after him, but he made the first down. Some other guys missed him, had a shot at him on that play. If he goes down, they don't score. That's on me."

Mark Kelso was one of the guys who Ingram got by. "On that big third-down play we played a drop zone," Kelso said ruefully, "so he was open when we should have had somebody in that zone, and that created a lot of extra space. I was playing deep middle and I came up and he put a move on me and I missed him. And somebody else missed him. And Darryl Talley ended up making the tackle. They ended up scoring on that drive. That's the margin of victory."

"You can't say a game is won or lost on one play," Talley said. "But that's one I'd like to have back."

And the Hostetler safety? "Those were two big plays," Talley said. "Don't take anything away from them. We just didn't make the key plays when we had to. And we don't win."

After a long and strenuous season, as all NFL campaigns are, a player's body begins to heal and recover from the hundreds of damaging hits, but the mental anguish lingers and takes much longer to diminish—if it ever does completely. "You're numb and hurt," Talley said. "You're out there for only one thing: to win the Super Bowl. That was the goal. The goal wasn't just to get there; the goal was to win it. What else is there?"

On their end the Giants needed to win two titanic games to earn their second Super Bowl championship. One in San Francisco against a Niners team chasing history, a third straight Super Bowl championship, and the other in Tampa against a Bills team that was one of the most explosive in its era. "Both of those games could have gone either way," Parcells said recently. "I think in both of those games we played about as well as we could have played and as hard as we could play. And the players did a great job of executing what we were trying to do. And I think what we were trying to do was really the only way we had a chance to win those games."

What greater tribute can a coach pay his team and their opponent? We played as hard as we could and we performed as well as we had hoped. It took everything we had to win the game.

Jim Ritcher wonders to this day if maybe the Bills weren't too self-assured when they arrived in Tampa. "To beat the Raiders like we did," he recalled, "maybe it gave us too much confidence. Just to be able to win like we did really boosted our confidence to go down there to Tampa. I think we played well down there. It was a well-played game. I don't remember any turnovers down there. But we didn't play our game."

There had not been a single turnover in the game, the first time ever in a Super Bowl. There were simply a number of big plays that got away from the Bills. "You have to put it behind you," Wright said, "and you have to get focused and go after it again."

During those winter months and into the spring, and even into training camp, that was the hardest part to reconcile: that as hard as it was to get there, it was going to be just as hard to get back. Jim Kelly remembers how difficult that was to overcome: "Because when you really think about it, you have to go through the whole offseason, knowing you didn't win it and then go back and do it again. And for us the work ethic's got to be there, not just within yourself but among every person on your football team. Everybody has to have that same work ethic. There can't be one or two guys who decide they're gonna take this offseason off, not quite work as hard as they did, or focus as much as they did, or [prepare] themselves physically for the next year. And for us the physical part was always there. We had talent. We had people who wanted to win."

Don Beebe arrived in Buffalo in 1989, a third-round draft pick. He was a wide receiver from an unknown college, Chadron State in Nebraska, who caught the attention of NFL scouts when he ran a blistering 4.25 in the 40-yard dash at the scouting combine. "I don't ever remember a time when guys weren't talking about going to the Super Bowl," he said. "When I got to Buffalo, this was already ingrained. From Polian to Levy, everybody from the secretary to the janitor to all your players, you got everybody thinking one common goal. 'We're going to the Super Bowl and we're going to win the Super Bowl.' And that's the way Buffalo was. I mean even the fans bought in."

More than anyone else, it was Kelly who had brought them together—not just on the field, but especially on all those Sunday nights when he opened his home to everyone. Polian still marvels at his quarterback's generosity. "It was not just the players," Polian said. "It was everybody in the organization. The wives of the coaches and all the administrators and even the scouts bonded with the wives of the players. The Wives Association was a big deal, run by them. It wasn't run by the Bills organization, so they all became friendly and worked together on community projects. So they all knew each other. And there weren't club seats in those days, so all the wives sat together on the 50-yard line in the lower deck. And they all got to know each other and helped each other out. So when a new player came in, the wives would band together and help her out, help get them relocated, get the children situated in school, things of that nature. It's a cliché, but it was one big family."

The coach wanted his players to relax the day before a game, so it was not uncommon on Saturdays to see the locker room fill up with wives and kids and friends. On Sundays, the atmosphere wasn't all that much different.

"We'd still be doing our work, getting ready for the game, but there were a lot of people guys would bring around," Kelso said. "Marv was very accommodating. Guys in television, writers, they'd be allowed in the locker room before the game. They had access as well and they benefitted from it. They developed close relationships with the guys."

Marv Levy misses Sundays the most. "Gameday," he remembered with a chuckle. "I used to tell our players, 'You don't get paid for Sundays. You get paid for preparing.' I enjoyed the association with the people. The fact—am I getting paid for this? A lifetime of being in a game I've always loved with people whom I admired. And as a coach maybe you can shape in the right direction the life and the character of the people you're responsible to work with. Those were very gratifying things."

If the Bills were like one big family, then their fans were like distant cousins, spread out in different directions but always looking out for you, always on hand for the big Sunday gatherings at the stadium. "You're kind of living in a fishbowl because it's such a small town, and everybody knows who all the players are," Pete Metzelaars said with a laugh. "I'm six foot eight, bright red hair. I kind of stand out in a crowd. Some of the guys on the team call me the fan magnet because obviously it's very hard for me to blend in with the crowd. People would see me and then they'd notice whoever I'm out with. So people would come up and ask for autographs, take pictures, *could you do this, could you do that* kind of stuff."

Metzelaars, like most of his teammates, took it all in stride. To a man they understood how much they meant to Buffalo. "They talk about football 365 days of the year," Metzelaars said, "because they're so interested, because they're so enamored, because they're so fascinated. It's a great opportunity to do a lot of good things for people because they're willing to come out and see you, donate money to whatever causes you might have, and take the opportunity to try to help other people less fortunate than you."

During the offseason the players would pile into a couple of cars and drive to high schools across western New York to play basketball games and raise money for charities. One night they even drew a crowd at the University of Rochester, where they played the team of old Boston Celtics star Jo Jo White. "I just loved those times," Beebe said. "And Jo Jo was a little up in age and he didn't play a lot and he assembled a team that had some great college players—and we beat them. Gale Gilbert [the third-string quarterback], I think he made 13 threes that night."

Thirteen threes? That's Beebe's story, and he's sticking to it.

Guys like Keith McKeller and Metzelaars had played basketball in college, and legend has it that Steve Tasker, only 5'9", could dunk. "Tasker could do this behind-the-head dunk that was just spectacular," Beebe said. "It brought the place to its feet."

Jerry Sullivan, *The Buffalo News* columnist, couldn't get over Tasker's athletic abilities. "I remember seeing him reverse-dunk a basketball at a charity basketball game," he wrote. "The guy is remarkable. If there were a contest for best all-around athlete in Buffalo over the past decade, he'd win it. As a high school senior in Kansas, he won the state title in the 100, 200, and long jump."

Sullivan likely saw Tasker and the other Bills the night they filled the Canisius College gym for a fund-raiser organized by J.D. Hill, an old Buffalo wide receiver from the 1970s. Tickets cost five dollars, and all the money went to aid Hill's Catch the Vision organization, which helps youngsters avoid and overcome drug and alcohol addictions by taking part in sports camps. Hill, who battled a chemical dependency himself, was determined "to get a strong message across to young men and women about the harmful effects of drugs and alcohol."

The Bills would play against PTAs and local media personalities—anyone for a worthy cause, Talley recalled. "We were like the Harlem Globetrotters. We looked like them, only we didn't play like them," he said.

Not that it mattered to anyone who attended. They were getting to spend more time watching their Bills. "And then," Beebe said, "we'd go to the nearest place to have Buffalo wings on the way home and just hang out."

"We were part of the fabric of western New York, there's no question," Kelso said. "We'd go to the Mason's Club or the Kiwanis Club and have a drink afterward with those guys, our fans. And they'd want to talk about the Super Bowl." Their fans were able to get up close and personal with them, able to let them know just how hard they took the loss, too, eager to let them know they would always have their back. "So we'd go over the game with them," Kelso remembers, and he would tell them, "we just didn't play as well as we were capable of playing. I know Jim threw a lot of passes, maybe we should have run more, and they controlled the ball way too much. There's no telling why we didn't play our best on that day. We played well, but well isn't good enough sometimes."

Talley never forgot one of his father's inspirational sayings: "My dad always told me, 'If it didn't kill you, it was going to make you stronger.' It was a tough defeat, a tough defeat to accept. But I had to say, 'We got to this game. We lost. We're going to come back, and no matter what they say or anybody thinks, we're going to win. I got one mind-set, and that's to win.' And that was it. If you're not willing to endure the pain that goes with it, you'll never go back."

Football is a game in which players get knocked down on every play, and then they have to get right back up and play on. And as wearing as that is on one's body, it is even more draining on one's psyche. "You're conditioned to get back up," Kelso said. "Marv had conditioned us to play each play. There are plays that go well and plays that go badly. You have to play each play. You can't worry about one play. That's the beauty of the NFL and football.

It's a team sport, and there are so many plays to be made. The more good plays you make, you're gonna win. But that doesn't always hold true."

As summer approached in 1991, the Bills became even more anxious to return to training camp, to begin another long march to the Super Bowl. While they accepted the fact that the Giants had controlled the game and the clock and made enough big plays to win the Super Bowl, the Bills did not believe the Giants were a better team. The only way to ease the burden of that one-point loss was to get back to the Super Bow—and come back with a win.

That was months down the road, and there was certainly no guarantee the Bills would be making a return trip, this time to Minneapolis on the final Sunday of the season, but that was the mission. Each time they took the field, whether in practice or on gameday, payback and revenge and redemption and all those other chestnuts clearly motivated them and commanded their attention.

As a teenager who grew up in Pittsburgh rooting for the Steelers, a dynasty that won four Super Bowls in six years, Kelso remembered the frustration—and ensuing determination—of the Houston Oilers and their coach, Bum Phillips, who were always denied a gateway to the Super Bowl by those great Steelers teams. "Bum Phillips would always say, 'Next year we're gonna knock the door down,'" Kelso said. "That's how we felt. And that's the feeling I felt. We were supremely confident we were going to go back that second year and that we were going to finish the deal. We were totally upbeat."

CHAPTER 7 | Marv Levy's Guiding Hand

WHEN THE BILLS arrived at training camp in the summer following their first Super Bowl, Marv Levy knew the biggest challenge his team had to confront was putting the wrenching loss to the Giants behind them. While the fear of losing can be tremendously motivating, it can also be paralyzing.

Defeat is always hard to accept because it is always unexpected. Your offensive plays and defensive alignments are designed to be successful. You practice and play to win. You enjoy the victory and then you move on to the next game filled with satisfaction and buoyed confidence. But when you lose and when you lose in such a disheartening way, it is only natural to wonder what the point was to all that hard work and effort.

After a lifetime spent in football, Levy knew only too well that "the devastation you feel after a loss is much more intense than the tremendous elation you experience after a victory. You pour everything into it, so a defeat stings that much more." Always a student of the game, Levy found wisdom in the words of another old coach, Duffy Daugherty, who had worked the sideline decades earlier at Michigan State: "If you don't learn anything from losing, there is no sense losing."

Levy and his team had suffered other difficult losses, certainly—most notably a playoff game in Cleveland at the end of the 1989 season that prevented them from reaching a second straight AFC Championship Game. Nevertheless, his young team had come back from that tough game in Cleveland, an outcome that had been sealed when a Buffalo receiver dropped a certain game-winning touchdown pass from Jim Kelly in the closing seconds.

What the old coach learned that day—Levy was 64 at the time—was that his two-minute offense, under the direction of his swashbuckling quarterback, Kelly, all but overcame a 10-point deficit in the fourth quarter. Kelly seemed to blossom in that situation and thrived on the intensity and pressure and pace of running an offense without a huddle, which limited a defense's ability to substitute players and call proper alignments. "We learned from that loss in Cleveland," Levy said. "We were down big at the start of the fourth quarter and we said, 'We can't wait to get into our two-minute drill. Let's go into it now.' And we did. Jim was perfect for it. He was fearless."

Passing on virtually every down, repeatedly hooking up with Thurman Thomas, who kept sliding around and behind Cleveland's defenders, the Bills cut the deficit to 34–30, only to watch Scott Norwood slip during his extra-point attempt and misfire. Suddenly a field goal and the specter of overtime was gone. There were four minutes left to play. Buffalo needed a touchdown to win. Then, in a prelude of what was to come on Super Bowl Sunday in Tampa, the Bills got the ball back with a little more than two minutes remaining in need of a big drive to win the game.

The scoreboard clock in Cleveland showed two minutes and 41 seconds remaining with the ball on the Buffalo 26-yard line, 74 yards from the end zone Kelly and the Bills desperately had to reach. On their previous drive, Kelly took the Bills 77 yards. Could he do it again? Buffalo had one timeout remaining along with the two-minute warning that would stop the clock. So the Bills went into their two-minute drill for the last time that day. Kelly stepped back a few yards from his center, Kent Hull. He would be in the shotgun formation now, ready to throw on every down. Not a second to waste.

Kelly would call the plays. The game was in his hands. One more touchdown drive and they'd be playing the next Sunday with a trip to the Super Bowl on the line. There was no doubt; the Bills just knew they were going to win. Or so they thought.

Two passes to Ronnie Harmon opened the drive and gave Buffalo a first down at its own 42 as the clock stopped for the two-minute warning. Then on fourth-and-10, Kelly found Don Beebe for 17 yards and a first down at the Cleveland 41. The Browns called timeout and tried to regroup. With a little more than a minute remaining, Kelly connected with Thomas for nine yards and another first down. Once more Cleveland called time-out. It seemed nothing could stop the Bills now. Not even another fourth-and-10 could end Buffalo's season as Kelly went to Andre Reed for just more than 10 yards. First down on the Cleveland 22. With 34 seconds on the clock, Kelly spiked the ball. Then he hit Thomas for 11 more yards and spiked the ball again.

Fourteen seconds and 11 yards to go. On the next play, Kelly found Harmon cutting across the back of the end zone, free and clear of any Cleveland defensive back. He was all by himself, no one even near him, and the pass from Kelly was perfect. It hit Harmon right in his hands and…the receiver dropped it.

There was time for one last play, but this time the Cleveland defense held. They were all over Kelly as he lofted one desperate heave toward Thomas breaking across the middle of the end zone on a post pattern. Instead the ball fell into the hands of a linebacker, Clay Matthews (father and namesake of the current Green Bay standout), who made the catch that Harmon could not.

Years later Kelly still understood the magnitude of that game: "I think that game was the turning point for our team. It didn't turn out quite the way we wanted. We went right down the field, and there was that pass that was right there, and it was dropped. And on the next play, I threw an interception. But Coach Marchibroda and Coach Levy had enough confidence, not just in me calling all the plays, but in all the people we had around us being smart enough to run a quick-paced offense."

Maybe no one was smarter than Hull. Decades later Steve Tasker would tell Peter King of *Sports Illustrated* how in tune he and Kelly had been: "Someone figured out once that, on average, there were 16 seconds between every play in our no-huddle offense. Jim would be able to look over the defense and call the formation we'd get in and make the play call. Then Kent would figure out our blocking assignments and call them out just before Jim would get the snap. Sometimes, Kent would know Jim had made the wrong call for the defense they had out there. Once, Jim got down to get his hands between Kent's legs for the snap, and there was Kent, turning his head around from his stance, shaking his head, like, 'No, no, no.' And Jim would change the play call. And it got done. No big deal. It just got done."

"It was exciting, knowing many people couldn't stop us when we were clicking on all cylinders," Kelly said. "It just tired defenses out. They couldn't get off the field. That's where the K-Gun started: a two-minute drill that we could run all the time.

And you had to have a great defense to do it because they weren't going to get much rest on the sideline."

"There was no surprise element to it," Kelly said. "We were going faster pace, throw it down the field. But look what I had around me. Thurman Thomas in the backfield. Andre Reed and James Lofton and Don Beebe, our three-wide-receiver package. And we had a great offensive line. We knew it would work because it worked against our defense in practice. When guys like Bruce Smith and Cornelius Bennett and Darryl Talley are having trouble stopping it, you're pretty confident it's going to work in games."

Not surprisingly, it made the Bills a better team on both sides of the line of scrimmage. There was no rest for the weary. "It made us a better conditioned team," Levy says. "It made our practices sharper, crisper. You had to be quick and fast to run it."

Thus began their championship march. Those two long, 70-yard drives out of the K-Gun late in the game at Cleveland and the big defensive stands down the stretch gave the Bills a confidence they never had before. Bennett walked off the field in Cleveland thinking, "'We have something special,'" he said. "People remember that game as the dropped pass. That was just one play in the game. We realized how close we had come. We realized we could have something special for a long time. Bill Polian just told us to trust in ourselves."

The Bills had struggled through the 1989 season, and it appeared they needed to win two of their last three games to reach the playoffs. They lacked the cohesion that great teams possess. Something was missing. Sure, they had a roster filled with famous names like Jim Kelly, Bruce Smith, and Thurman Thomas, but there were groups of players, small circles of friends, that left some longing for a genuine sense of camaraderie.

"Jim—and to a certain extent Thurman Thomas, Cornelius Bennett and Darryl Talley—they weren't in the mix. They weren't real good buddies," Tasker said. "They were immensely talented. Three of those guys were future Hall of Famers, but they weren't real good buddies. We got to the last three games of that '89 season and we needed to win two of them to control our own destiny and something happened in those last three games. Then something palpable happened. I didn't know what it was until later. We started to play for each other. Mostly Jim and Bruce—they started to pull for each other. They started to watch each other play. They stood up on the sideline. They'd pat each other on the back when they came off the field—little things like that. And we did not win two of those three games, but things fell our way and we still made it into the playoffs.

"The game in Cleveland was one of the great games ever that people really talk about. Our guy, Ronnie Harmon, dropped a pass in the corner of the end zone that would have won it, and next play Jim threw a pick to Clay Matthews. But we really felt like we came together that day. That game was epic."

The old coach could see his team was coming together on the field—and just as important—off the field. It was something he had waited to see for a long time and it harkened back to a conversation he once had with his general manager. Levy remembered, "One comment Bill Polian made resonated with me: 'It's amazing what you can accomplish when no one gets the credit, and no one cares who gets the credit.' And that's the way we functioned in the organization. It was total organization counts."

The Cleveland playoff game had become a watershed game for the Bills. Although some players had spent time together away from the playing field in previous years, playing charity basketball games and hunting, they all made a commitment to stay close that winter. It may have been just a bunch of guys hanging out, chilling in upstate New York, but they became more than just a football team.

During the season "You're spending 16 hours a day with these guys. All the time. You're constantly around each other. You're like brothers. We needed to connect like that after the season," Talley remembered. "A lot of the guys would hunt together in the early years, and [later] a bunch of us would go around and play basketball games together for charity more and more."

Dennis DiPaolo remembers how the locals tried to go head-to-head with the Bills and were determined to beat them in some of those charity basketball games. "I remember our Erie Lackawanna game with the media," he said. "And the media came out and they really wanted to play hard. And we're thinking, *Are you kidding? Are you really trying to beat up Jim Kelly? How are you going to box out Pete Metzelaars?* You know, Pete Metzelaars is a great basketball player anyhow and he's huge, six foot eight."

The Bills hardly took these games seriously, but they realized it was actually fun rubbing shoulders, and trading elbows, with their fans. Now, after the 1989 season, they were making it a point to see more of each other, to bond as a team. "We'd go to movies, go bowling together," Talley said. "If one guy had an event, a golf outing or something, the next thing you'd know we had 10, 12 guys there. Whenever anybody wanted to do something, all he had to do was tell one or two guys and then you'd get 20 or 25. *Where are we going? Just tell me where to go?*"

If the players needed to blow off steam, then Buffalo provided the perfect remedy: snowmobiling. And they were willing to go outside their ranks if anyone had the nerve to ride with them. "They really got into that," DiPaolo said. "That was always a lot of fun, wild times. You'd get 20 guys and they'd go, 'Dennis, you can ride Thurman's. Thurman can't go.' Everyone had them. So we're out snowmobiling, and the trails are hard to see, and they just say, 'Hey, follow the leader', and everybody lines up.'" They were like a bunch of NASCAR drivers, taking their positions in the snow with Kelly pretty much always commanding the pole position.

"We're all going at a nice pace," DiPaolo says, "about 20 of us, and you know Jim, he's gotta be first in line and *boom,* he takes off. It was a special time with those guys. When we were done, the celebration would continue. And they'd tell you about these ridges and cliffs we just went over, about three feet wide, and I said, 'We didn't really go over that, did we?' Thank goodness I never looked down. 'We didn't want to tell you,' they'd say. I could have gone down those cliffs 300 feet, and they go, 'Yeah.' Chestnut Ridge. Cliffs on each side, and the ridge is about three feet wide. Snow from December to March, snowmobiling got really popular. Everybody got snowmobiles."

Even in the snow, Frank Reich took a backseat to Kelly. "One time I'm snowmobiling with Jim and I totaled his snowmobile," Reich said. "I went around a curve in a park, and we're going about 100 miles per hour or something stupid and I'm trying to race Jim and I go around this snow bank and I lose traction and there was this huge boulder—I mean *huge* boulder—and I'm going right at it and I'm gonna crash into it and I'm probably gonna die. About five feet from the boulder I just bailed. I just jumped off the snowmobile, and it crashed. It just totaled the snowmobile. We did some crazy stuff. *I* did some crazy stuff.

"We had fun on the practice field. We had fun playing games. We had fun off the field," Reich continued. When the snow began to melt, their attention turned to golf. "We kind of bounced around all over the place," Metzelaars said. "We played a lot of public courses. Some country clubs, even if you weren't a member you could get out because you were playing for the Buffalo Bills. Those perks were nice."

By the time spring awakened, they were anxious for summer, to get back on the field, to set their sights on a Super Bowl win that had been within their grasp. Not since the end of January, when Levy convened the final meeting of the 1990 team, had all of them been together. Levy had taken that loss to the Giants as hard as anyone. He had felt nothing but "devastation" as he made his way back to the hotel late that Sunday night, where his wife and daughter were waiting for him in tears. He tried to dry their eyes and tried to force himself to sleep, but he kept replaying all the big plays in the game over and over again, an endless loop, all through the night—"pounding the mattress" as he put it. Finally, near daybreak, he remembered an old sonnet from a book of poetry his mother had given him when he joined the Army Air Corps in 1943. An old Scottish warrior, Sir Andrew, had written: "A little I'm hurt but not yet slain. I'll just lie down and bleed awhile and then I'll rise and fight again."

Upon returning to Buffalo after the Super Bowl he shared those lines with his players before they departed into the offseason. He left the poetry to Sir Andrew and then spoke in plain terms to his men. "There were no pep talks," Levy said. "It wasn't fire and brimstone. We owned up honestly. *What could we do better?* By own up, some of them already said it. *Yeah, I missed a tackle. Yes, I dropped a ball.* In other words don't agonize over your performance."

For days and weeks, Levy remained haunted by the defeat. If he had a chance to do it all over again, would it have mattered if he had done anything differently? "We spent too much time getting tickets for our family during the week," he suggested, groping for answers. "When we got to the Super Bowl site, were we too taken up with the excitement of it rather than focusing on practicing? Things of that nature. It was a very close game. People are always pointing to the fact that the Giants had 40 minutes of possession to our 20. What about that? Well, in the close games we played all year, that was the story of the no-huddle offense. We'd be off the field in a split second. Finally, I just felt, let's go back to work."

Looking back, Levy said, "That was the day I started getting them ready for the next season. It wasn't a matter of a planned pep talk. There wasn't a 'starting point.'"

It turned out more than a few players requested copies of the poem. It would serve as their battle hymn through hard times, beginning with those days immediately following their trip to Tampa. It was part of a five-step program the coach instilled: mourn, own up, recognize the good, make a plan, and go to work. "We went through that period of mourning," Levy said. "And I know the pain we were all feeling. I said, 'It's going to take some hard work. You're a great bunch of guys, and the hill you're going to have to climb is going to be very steep. But take it game by game, and we've got to prepare for next season and get some rest. Get going. Get refreshed. Let's get going down the road again.'"

When the Bills arrived at training camp in July 1991, Levy saw no reason to address his men any differently than he had in any other summer. Having been to one Super Bowl, he knew they were determined to get to the next one. They didn't need any fiery pep talk. This was no movie. "Marv was masterful at knowing the right buttons to push," Reich said. "You never got a canned speech from Marv. He doesn't have anything canned about him. He's a very smart, creative guy, a very personable guy who had a unique talent of understanding players and what buttons to push individually and then bringing it all together. I think that's truly one of his great qualities."

Marv Levy had grown up in Chicago, Notre Dame country, especially in those days of the Depression and World War II before the NFL made it big. And he knew something about the way Knute Rockne was portrayed on film. "You know the movie *Knute Rockne All-American?* You know how Rockne's portrayed?" Levy asked, his voice rising. "'We're gonna do this, and they're gonna do that, and this, this, this.' Growing up in my neighborhood, there were some guys who played on Knute Rockne's teams. They said that movie, that wasn't Rockne, that was Pat O'Brien the actor. Rockne wasn't doing that. That wasn't Rockne at all.

"I don't believe in pep talks. To me, most pep talks are just noise. If there's something that resonates at the right time, I think it comes through. There are some things that are inspirational, but they have to be genuine. And once in a while, I would talk to our team and use a scene from history, and there'd be some application of what they were doing that day and I hoped it would resonate."

Occasionally he would tell them a story he had heard from his father, who had served in the Marines during World War I. The troops were exhausted from battle, and their commander was about to lead them into another attack, proclaiming: "When it's too tough for them, it's just right for us." That one worked in the heat and humidity of Miami or the snow and ice of Buffalo. Sometimes he would employ Winston Churchill, whom he regarded as the greatest historical figure of the 20th century, his idol who would not accept defeat. As a young boy he would listen on the radio to Churchill's inspirational talks "to the British people who were all but defeated." Or he would invoke Ben Franklin, who said, "Failing to prepare is preparing to fail."

Levy himself was not given to hyperbole. Upon graduating from high school in Chicago, he enlisted in the Army Air Corps and spent the rest of World War II in uniform. He was dismissive of those who used military and combat metaphors to describe football games and inspire players. Once, in reference to the Super Bowl, he said, "This is not a must-win. World War II was a must-win."

After the war Levy went to Coe College in Iowa and then earned a master's degree in English history from Harvard. He then embarked on his long ascent up the coaching ranks from a high school assignment and on to college campuses at the University of New Mexico, the University of California at Berkeley, and William and Mary.

Finally, in 1969, Levy arrived in the NFL as a kicking teams coach for the Philadelphia Eagles. The next year George Allen made him the special teams coach for the Los Angeles Rams. Levy was also part of the staff Allen assembled a year later in Washington with the Redskins. From there Levy made his way to the Canadian Football League, where he was the head coach of the Montreal Alouettes for five seasons during which he won two Grey Cup championships.

In 1978 Levy returned to the NFL as head coach of the Kansas City Chiefs, where he spent five years. Despite making steady improvement, Levy was fired after the strike-shortened 1982 season when the Chiefs fell to 3–6. After taking a two-year sabbatical he spent a season with the Chicago Blitz of the USFL before

Polian fired Buffalo coach Hank Bullough in the middle of the 1986 season and recruited Levy to replace him.

Polian had known Levy since his first years in football, when Polian had served as a part-time personnel scout for the Alouettes. He was captivated by how self-effacing the coach was. After all, this was in an era when Vince Lombardi's fiery persona was the gold standard of coaching. And when Polian made it to Kansas City as a scout, he was immediately awestruck by the manner in which Levy handled his team.

In those years the Chiefs and Houston Oilers would meet in a rookie scrimmage, a big opportunity for a young player to make his mark. One day before the scrimmage, at the end of practice, Levy gathered all his rookies around him and had them kneel down on the grass so he could tell them something important: "Listen, for many of you, this is your chance to show if you can play in the National Football League. And you've put in a lot of work in these past two weeks, and we want you to have a chance to do your best. I want everybody to have a chance to show what they can do. Not everybody will make it, but everybody should have the opportunity to give it their best. What I want you to do is to make sure that you packed your turf shoes for tomorrow's scrimmage. Don't forget to do it because Arrowhead Stadium is on turf, and we've been practicing here on grass for the past couple of weeks. I want you to really have a chance to do your best. If you don't have the right shoes on, you won't do your best."

Polian was standing not far from Levy, thinking, "My God what a way to get that message across. This is the greatest communicator I've ever come across in my life."

Their association continued when they hooked up with the Blitz, "an expansion team who lost its owner before the season ever began, before we left training camp, and we were a wart of the league," Polian said. "And we kept on driving and working hard and we kept on being levelheaded and doing all the things that Marv Levy teams do. We ended up winning, I think, five of our last six games after effectively turning the whole team over during the course of the season. So there was no question in my mind, none, that when we were going to make a coaching change in Buffalo that Marv Levy would take us to the top. No question whatsoever. That's what I told Mr. Wilson. 'Mr. Wilson, I'd bet all the money I have in the world, or will ever make, that Marv Levy can take us to the top.'"

Ralph Wilson was well aware of Levy's work in the NFL. When the call came, Levy got in his car and drove down to Buffalo "as fast as I could go within the speed limit." However, he did lie about his age. Levy was 61 when the Bills hired him and he remembers being asked at his first press conference if he was too old to handle the job. "They asked me my age, and I said 57," Levy loved to say in later years. "It just sounded younger." The aging coach was more than up to the task, but he always felt a little silly about not being more forthcoming. Deep down and well into his 80s, he always believed it didn't matter how old you are; what counted was what you did, what you accomplished.

From the first time Polian saw Levy address his team, the general manager knew he had hired the right man to rally the Bills. "He talked about what it takes to win is simple and easy," Polian recalled.

"We need to be a team," Levy told his players. "We need to do things together, to take care of the little things because from them big things grow, so details are important. And acknowledge our rules around here. I have three rules: be a good citizen, be on time, and give your best all the time. Now let's go win a game."

"And he got a standing ovation,' Polian said. "The players stood up and cheered because he was such a phenomenal communicator. He broke the game down into very simple pieces that they could understand."

Success did not come overnight. Levy guided the Bills to only two wins in their final seven games of the 1986 season. Then in 1987, his first full season as their head coach, he produced a 7–8 record in a season that was disrupted by a players' strike and the use of replacement players, "scabs," for three games. In his third year in Buffalo, he was finally piloting a full 16-game season and he guided the Bills to a 12–4 record and the AFC East title. One of Levy's big maxims was "Don't beat yourself. Don't do dumb things. Don't commit penalties."

"So he boiled it down to a catch phrase: 'Don't be dumb and don't be dirty.' So we're out practicing one day. It's early October, and a defensive back, a scout team guy, makes a really dumb play, interferes with a receiver and knocks him down. And I'm standing on the sideline, and there are some veteran defensive players standing there, and about three voices yell, 'Hey, don't be dumb and don't be dirty!'" Polian said he was so excited he couldn't wait to go over and tell his coach, "They get it. They get the message. You got through to them. They know what's important." The memory still brings a smile to Polian's face. "And to this day if you ask them how to be a smart player they'll tell you, don't be dumb and don't be dirty."

Levy was cut from a different cloth than most football coaches. He was a trim man with gray hair that he kept cropped fairly short. He bore an inquisitive look that belied his intellect. He looked like an Ivy League professor and he liked to get his message across in a calm, straightforward manner without histrionics as if he were giving a lecture. He was far from a yeller or a screamer.

"He was the most inspirational—in a low-key, understated, non-ego way—coach I'd ever seen in my life," Polian said. "And he had a phenomenal sense of humor. We had the Awards Assembly every Monday after we'd win a game. That's what he called it, the Awards Assembly. And we would give out the hokiest of awards: two tickets to a movie, dinner for two at a local restaurant. It wasn't thousands of dollars. These things couldn't have been more than $50 tops. And he'd give out sacks of popcorn, big huge garbage-size bags for anybody who got a sack. And if Jeff Wright and Bruce Smith shared a sack they would argue over who should get the popcorn sack. *No, that was my sack. No way, that was my sack.* And Marv would say, 'All right, all right, all right. I'll make an executive decision here. You can both have one.' And everybody would cheer.

"It was those things that he did that allowed everybody to be part of it, as he said, the whole is greater than the sum of its parts. And they believed that. And he believed it. Everybody in the organization believed it. We lived by his dictums. We can recite them to this day. I've been with him for 25 years, and he's my mentor in all things football and most in life, simply the greatest teacher any of us have ever been around. And because of what he taught and what he was and how he viewed the game and the team and life, he created this atmosphere where everybody thrived."

Indeed, it wasn't long before Levy and the Bills started to find their way. A strong nucleus was in place, and Polian was only making the Bills stronger with deft deal-making for Bennett and strong drafts that brought Shane Conlon and Thomas to Buffalo.

Bennett had been instrumental in one of the titanic trades in NFL history. An outside linebacker from the University of Alabama, Bennett had been the second overall pick in the 1987 draft by the Indianapolis Colts, but he could not come to terms with the Colts. Bennett's holdout lasted 102 days, right before the trading deadline on Halloween, when the Colts, Los Angeles Rams, and Bills reached their summit accord. The Colts organized the complex transaction that sent Bennett to Buffalo for the Bills' first-round draft picks in 1988 and 1989 and their 1989 second-round pick along with running back Greg Bell. Indianapolis then contributed their first and second-round draft picks in 1988, their No. 2 pick in 1989, and a running back, Owen Gill, to the Los Angeles Rams for the running back who broke O.J. Simpson's single season rushing record, Eric Dickerson.

Bennett commanded a $3.9 million contract with Buffalo, which included a $1.4 million signing bonus. "I was traded Halloween Day of 1987," Bennett remembered of the day he hit pay dirt. "The Saturday before the Bills would play the Redskins. Darryl Talley hurt his neck in that game. And when I arrived at the locker room on Monday morning at 7:00 AM to meet with the coaches and learn the new defenses, he had already come in to see the trainer and get treatment. After I met with the coaches, I was sitting on a stool at my locker, and Darryl came over and sat next to me. The first thing he told me: 'Put the playbook away. I'll teach you everything you need to know.' Just like that. Before my first game, guys were taking me out, teaching me the ropes. I felt like I had been with them forever."

If Smith ever had any doubt how much a defensive star was worth, all he had to do now was look across the locker room. And motivation was a concern early in Smith's career. "He struggled for the first two years," Polian said. "He struggled with his weight. He struggled with the system. He struggled adapting to pro football. And there was some inside the building who even thought about trading him. Mr. Wilson, to his credit, stayed firm and Bruce developed into a Hall of Famer. But the first couple of years were not good."

In the summer of 1989, Smith was able to cash in. He had played out the contract he had signed as the No. 1 overall pick in the 1985 draft. He was a free agent and he was vehement in his demand to become the highest-paid defensive player in the game.

The Denver Broncos were eager to enrich Smith with $7.5 million over five years, surpassing the $1 million per season the Bills had offered. Smith said the Bills should pass and let him go to Denver and take the two first-round draft picks that would be accorded to Buffalo. But Polian understood Smith's true value. He was just as a valuable to the defense as Kelly was to the offense. And so Smith became the highest paid defensive player in the NFL and the second highest paid Buffalo Bill behind Kelly.

Smith was difficult to contain on the gridiron, and his personality off the field was just as challenging. He would miss stretches of training camp, saying his knee was bothering him. More than one teammate thought that was a dubious excuse. Even so, they realized he always showed up on gameday. Smith was even named the AFC's Defensive Player of the Year in 1987. But on the eve of the following season, he was hit with a 30-day suspension for violating of the league's substance abuse policy. He would sit out the first four games of the 1988 season. So concerned were the Bills about his association with a suspected drug dealer, they hired undercover detectives to shadow their All-Pro defensive end for three weeks.

The suspension rocked Buffalo, and Levy took it particularly hard. When he had come to the Bills he made it clear to Polian and John Butler, the director of player personnel, that they would "only bring people of high character to our team."

"And I didn't want to confuse that with personality," Levy said. "There were introverts, and there were guys who were extroverted, but no one with a previous history of drug abuse, no one who had been an addict or a problem. In some cases a suspension sends a guy the wrong way, and in some cases the right way. It resonated with Bruce. He owned up. As a coach you try to convey, you deserved it, so what do you do now to convince people that's not you or that's not going to be you. I hoped there'd be a message he'd see in it."

"When Bruce was suspended, that was a tough time for him, and that was a tough time for the team," Polian said, before channeling Levy. "But adversity is an opportunity for heroism. I'm sure you've heard that before. So we just accepted that and moved on."

But Smith didn't turn over a new leaf overnight. According to Bob Koshinski, "More than once Bruce was found sleeping at a stoplight after a few too many, and there were a number of [other] stories that never made the media. Ed Stillwell was in charge of security for the Buffalo Bills and he worked for Bill Polian. Ed had a lot of contacts, along with Vince Tobia, who was an attorney, also a former state trooper. They cleaned up a few situations that never made the media. Nothing serious, of course—that goes on in this day and age, but boys will be boys kind of things—more like traffic incidents, things like that. Nobody ever got hurt. But it would have been embarrassing news. But some of that stuff got squelched."

By 1991 the Bills were a seasoned and veteran team and had established themselves as the best team in their conference. They

125

had some great players who had been celebrated coming out of college, such as Kelly and Bennett and Smith, as well as some sleepers who were drafted in later rounds, such as Reed and Tasker. They all played hard and they played together and they were having the time of their life. "We loved to win. We loved to party. We loved to have fun," Kelly once put it.

"I don't know what goes on today in the NFL with some of these players, but that group partied hard during the week," Koshinski remembered. "Those guys, they weren't Boy Scouts. I mean, when they had a night off they'd go to some of the nightclubs."

As the Bills profile grew nationwide, they were treated like rock stars around Buffalo. More than a few of them enjoyed playing that role. After all several of them even had their own weekly television shows. Kochinski remembers, "More than once, they'd get out of the limo and they'd already had a couple of drinks before the show started, and I knew they were going for more afterward."

A night on the town in Buffalo might include stops at Mulligan's Brick Bar or the Pierce Arrow Bar and Grill—places with deafening sound systems and spacious dance floors. But during the week after practice, you could often find some of them at a local working-class hangout right near the stadium. "The Big Tree Inn, as much a neighborhood bar as you'd ever find, was a favorite hangout of those guys," Kochinski said. "They didn't need the limelight. They'd go to the Big Tree Inn—it's a very rural bar—and just hang with the guys. They weren't elitists. Let's put it that way. They didn't have to go to the swankiest joint in town. They adapted to Buffalo."

"It was a blue-collar town, and I'm a blue-collar guy," said Phil Hansen, a defensive end, effectively speaking for so many of his teammates. "You know, I'm not overly gifted in any kind of way. I just work hard like the community. I fit in great here."

Hansen had grown up hardscrabble poor in Oakes, North Dakota, a town of fewer than 2,000 residents, where he worked long hours on the family's farm. "My earliest recollection of football was being out there in the seventh grade, waiting with the other kids for practice to start," he would say years later, when he took his place on the Buffalo Bills Wall of Fame. "Kids were just saying, 'Gee, this stinks. It's hot. We just want to play the game.' And I'm just like, 'I'm glad to be here. If I were at home, I'd really be working.' I didn't even think I'd go to college. You know, kids kind of plan for this now, sending out tape in the eighth grade. I don't think we even had tape in 1986. But I fell through the cracks in a good way. I guess I just didn't know it any other way."

By the time all the Bills reported to training camp that summer, they knew how much work they needed to put in on the field and how to take it easy off the field. "This blows people's minds," Reich recalled. "We played 18 holes of golf every day in training camp right at Fredonia Country Club. We played nine holes after the morning practice and nine holes after the afternoon practice. Sometimes there was just four of us, sometimes there were 12 of us. Don Beebe and I, Shane Conlan and Gale Gilbert, Kent Hull and Will Wolford. It was Darryl Talley and Bruce Smith, Steve Tasker, and Pete Metzelaars. That was the main group. Occasionally we'd get Jim to come out there. That was kind of the core group. That's why we used to call it Club Marv because training camp was so easy."

"Marv really understood how to get the best out of the guys," Beebe said. "Some teams are different. Some teams, you can't allow those guys to go play golf because they're immature. Okay, they won't take practice seriously, they'll show up late, things like that. But that was a mature team. Marv made us understand, okay you can do what you want in the offseason, but when it's practice time you have to take it seriously. And we did. We did a ton of stuff together. And yet we practiced—and we practiced hard—and we understood what we needed to accomplish."

Still, starting over was never easy. They would enter the 1991 season with the same 0–0 record as the other 27 teams in the league. What's more, they knew every team they would go up against would bring their A game to best the defending AFC champions.

"It's so disappointing to lose a Super Bowl," Jim Ritcher says. "But to know we're all together and all the people, all our fans, were still behind us, that gave us the drive for the next year to go back. It was such a great experience to play for the Buffalo Bills and the people of that area. Our attitude was, let's get back to work and we can do this."

The next Super Bowl was six months away in Minneapolis. And they had every intention of being there.

CHAPTER 8 | Super Bowl XXVI

THE 1991 SEASON was about to get under way, and the media was beginning to call Thurman Thomas "the Thurmanator." However, unlike the superstrong cyborg Arnold Schwarzenegger portrayed on-screen with the aid of special effects, there was nothing manufactured about Thomas' game. He was a natural force of power and agility on the gridiron, a threat to score any time he ran with the ball or caught a pass.

If he had never received the recognition—read: adulation—that he felt he deserved, that certainly changed during the course of Super Bowl XXV. He put on a dazzling performance with the whole world watching. No player on either side performed better that night than Thomas. He rushed for 135 yards on 15 carries, an average of nine yards per carry against one of the most impenetrable defenses in football. His 31-yard touchdown gallop gave the Bills their final lead early in the fourth quarter. He also caught five passes for 55 additional yards. Nevertheless, the Super Bowl's Most Valuable Player Award went to a player on the winning team, the Giants' Ottis Anderson, another running back. Even Bill Parcells had to admit, "Thurman Thomas should have been the MVP."

To Thomas, this was just one more slight he had to put up with throughout his career, and when he returned to Giants Stadium in the summer of 1991 for a preseason game, he inscribed a pointed message on the back of his shoes: SB XXV MVP. "I thought I outperformed everyone on the field that night," Thomas said. "After going through a whole offseason and into training camp, I still felt that way."

Thomas' problems with the media, with football really, went back to his days at Oklahoma State, where he ran for a career 4,500 yards and scored 43 touchdowns. He was so good that his teammate, another future Hall of Famer, Barry Sanders, had a hard time getting on the field. But in his senior year, Thomas injured his knee—not badly enough to jeopardize a career in football but damaging enough to hurt him in the draft.

His name was not called until the second round as the 40th player selected and the first player chosen by the Bills in 1988. Thomas has a TV tape of that draft day, showing him sitting in his living room, waiting…and waiting….and waiting. Disbelieving… seething…fuming. Teams around the league wondered about his surgically repaired right knee and had doubts about whether he could stand up to the rigors of the NFL. In college he had been such a workhorse that his coach rested him during the week, running him like a thoroughbred on Saturdays.

As the first round gave way to the second round, Bill Polian wondered if perhaps all those teams that had passed on Thomas knew something that he did not know. "We were thrilled he was still there, but we were also a little leery," Polian recalled. "Did they know something we didn't?"

Even after he made it to the big show and showed up all those teams who had passed him by in the draft—seven other running backs were chosen before him—he remained bitter. As a rookie, he watched the tape before each game. It was all the motivation he would ever need. Even years later, as he was about to begin his fourth season in the NFL, he still found himself watching that tape a couple of times a year—just to rev him up, just to get him going come gameday. He carried a chip on his shoulder that teams like the Los Angeles Rams, Atlanta Falcons, New Orleans Saints, and Houston Oilers—who had been talking to him often on the eve of the draft—gave him a cold shoulder come draft day.

"That was supposed to be the happiest day in my life," Thomas remembered, before explaining how the opinions added more fuel to his fire. "I've been proving people wrong all along. I wasn't supposed to be able to catch the ball coming out of college. I wasn't supposed to last this long with a supposedly bad knee. That's the way it is. I have to go out and just keep performing."

Not a big man, he carried nearly 200 pounds on his compact, 5'10" frame. He was capable of sudden and explosive bursts of speed and the ability to pivot away from defenders when he would make a catch. He did not show much emotion on the field, but he brought a lot of style to his game—and even more substance.

He also brought attitude. He bristled when Bills offensive coordinator Ted Marchibroda once told the media that Jim Kelly is "the Michael Jordan of this team."

"I think I am," Thomas quickly responded. "I guess we have two."

Thomas grew up in Missouri, Texas. An only child whose parents separated when he was five, his hero was Earl Campbell, a powerful running back who could carry his team—and literally the other team—on his back. That was how Thurman liked to picture himself—as the backbone of the Bills. He could be a brooding man. His tough demeanor masked his sensitivity and insecurity. In some fundamental ways he was like the place he played in: never fully accepted or appreciated the way bigger stars and cities are regarded.

But everyone around the league knew that if the Bills were going to make another serious run to the Super Bowl in the 1991 season, they were going to need another big effort from Thomas. He was an extremely versatile and talented player who could tip the balance of the game any time he touched the ball. It was no secret that one of the keys to stopping the Bills was stopping Thomas.

It was also no secret that from the moment they arrived at training camp, "Mission to Minneapolis" was Buffalo's mission statement. "Ever since we lost that game to the Giants, that's all that's been on my mind," Kelly said. "That Super Bowl defeat, there's not a more devastating feeling. It took me five months to stop thinking about it."

Going into the new season, the Bills' only real areas of concern were the physical conditions of Kelly and Bruce Smith. Kelly had sprained his ankle during a preseason game with the Green Bay Packers, and Smith underwent knee surgery in July and was expected to miss the first month of the season.

But Kelly was ready for Opening Day at home in Rich Stadium, and despite aggravating his ankle again in the third quarter, he remained in the game as the Bills went on to defeat Miami 35–31. Buffalo piled up 582 yards on offense, and Thomas ran up even more incredible numbers than he had in the Super Bowl: 165 yards on the ground, 103 more yards on receptions, and two touchdowns.

The Bills went on to win their next four games before coming up short on a Monday night in Kansas City, suffering through a 33–6 blowout to the Chiefs. Buffalo fumbled five times, and Kelly was sacked six times in the defeat. Bouncing right back the Bills went on a five-game winning streak before losing to a bad Patriots team in New England. Still, Thomas continued to excel, and the defense was getting stronger each week, even with a diminished Smith back on the field.

But Scott Norwood was having problems. In the fourth week of the season, in a game at Tampa Stadium (where he had missed from 47 yards in the Super Bowl) Norwood again lined up for a kick, this time from only 36 yards away and again watched the ball sail wide right. Nearly identical to his failure just months before, it was a sobering sight for the team and its fans. Then, in a late-season game in Los Angeles, with the Bills trying to secure home-field advantage throughout the playoffs, Norwood had a terrible day against the Raiders (the same Raiders that Buffalo had humiliated for the AFC title the previous season). In the second half of a taut game, Norwood missed three field goals and even blew an extra point, a grievous error, before Kelly led a late touchdown drive to pull the Bills within a point 27–26. Norwood then made the extra point and in overtime, following Mark Kelso's interception on the second play of sudden-death, he managed to make the game-winning field goal.

Despite their problems at kicker, the Bills entered the playoffs filled with confidence. Kelly had thrown for nearly 1,000 more yards and nine more touchdowns than he had in 1990. Cornelius Bennett had nine sacks, and Nate Odomes had five interceptions. But the real stalwart of the team was Thomas. He rushed for 1,407 yards and caught 62 passes for another 631 yards. His output, more than 2,000 yards of total offense, cemented his status as the nucleus of the Buffalo offensive attack.

At long last he was finally hearing the praise he had long desired. The NFL noticed, too, naming him its Most Valuable Player that season. "He's our big-play man," Kelly would say. "We had to find more ways to take advantage of him."

With Thomas leading the way, "the whole team got better," Kelly acknowledged. "Everybody asks us, 'How can you guys get any better?' We did it with each individual contributing."

Even if no one was willing to concede that Thurman was the Bulls' Michael Jordan—and really there was no player in football like Air Jordan—you could certainly claim that Thomas was the heart and soul of Buffalo. Finally, even Thomas had his vindication: he was the right man, in the right city, at the right time.

After earning a bye week in the playoffs, the Bills were anxious to get back on the road to the Super Bowl, anxious to face the Chiefs who had embarrassed them on *Monday Night Football*. It would be a different venue this time, a different story, and a different outcome. And Buffalo would have two of its best defensive forces back in the lineup, Smith and Jeff Wright, who had both been sidelined in their October meeting.

Kelly, who had rested his sore knee for three weeks coming into the game, came out throwing strikes. He promptly connected with Andre Reed for two quick touchdowns as Buffalo sprinted to a 24–0 lead. He then threw three interceptions, one setting up a Chiefs score. Still, the Bills won easily 37–14.

Norwood kicked three field goals in the game. And when he connected on his last kick, from 47 yards, he punctured the air with a tomahawk chop and made a thumbs-up gesture toward his opponents. It was almost as if he were finally exorcising the demons that had haunted him since his super miss. "I let my emotions out," Norwood said. Then he repeated an interviewer's question: "Do I think about the Super Bowl kick?" After a pause he answered, "Uh, not really. I mean, I think about the kick sometimes. I don't think I'll ever be able to forget it. But when you're on the field, you have to put it out of your mind. I can't change it. I'd like to put it behind me." The kick against the Chiefs, though not nearly as important, put an exclamation point on the day. "It felt good to be out there and contribute," Norwood said.

But it wasn't all good news for the Bills. Smith limped off the field in the third quarter; his left knee, which had been operated on that summer, had caused him persistent discomfort and pain throughout the season. He was questionable for the next Sunday's matchup with John Elway and the Denver Broncos for the AFC championship. And Smith wasn't the only unknown who had Marv Levy worried. Four offensive linemen were also nursing injuries—a major concern for the Bills high-octane scoring machine.

Against Denver, Levy's apprehension was more than realized. The Bills offense never got any traction, and the defenses ended up dominating the game. More than nine minutes into the second half, it remained a scoreless contest. Then Elway attempted a screen pass deep in his own territory. Nose tackle Wright managed to deflect the pass and Bills linebacker Carlton Bailey, blitzing on the play, picked it off and took it 11 yards into the end zone. Not long after, Elway left the game with a badly bruised thigh.

With only 4:18 left in the game, Norwood was able to negotiate the tricky winds to nail a 44-yard field goal. The Bills had a 10–0 lead, and a trip to Minneapolis seemed imminent. Then Elway's understudy, Gary Kubiak, playing in his final game before retiring, led the Broncos on the only touchdown drive of the game.

It covered 85 yards in eight plays, culminating with Kubiak scoring on a quarterback draw from the 3. Buffalo's lead was cut to three with less than two minutes remaining.

Denver promptly recovered an onside kick at midfield with 1:38 left and two timeouts remaining. Suddenly the Bills were in serious trouble. But on the next play, Kirby Jackson forced a fumble and recovered, and that pretty much sealed Buffalo's fate. The Bills managed to run off all but the final 17 seconds before relinquishing possession to the Broncos at the Denver 20-yard line. Two passes got them near midfield as time ran out, but it wouldn't be enough. Buffalo's unheralded defense had persevered.

As 80,000 fans left Rich Stadium, they knew the game could have easily swung Denver's way. Kicker David Treadwell missed all three field goals he tried: a 47-yarder that sailed wide left and two attempts from 42 and 37 yards that both hit the right upright. The Bills emerged by the skin of their teeth.

Still, in the joyous Buffalo locker room, Wright submitted, "If we play the way we did today, we should win the Super Bowl." His optimism was understandable. The defense had been dominant in both playoff games and, even though its stars were battered, Buffalo still possessed some of the biggest studs in the game, including Smith, Bennett, Shane Conlan, and Darryl Talley. Bennett, who had made nine sacks and 107 tackles during the season, basically shut down the Broncos' running game as he patrolled the field. And Smith, who had played through arthritic pain in his left knee all year, came through with his best game of the campaign. No one would benefit from a week off before the Super Bowl more than Smith, who needed to be in peak form if Buffalo were to stop the mighty Washington Redskins, easily the elite of the National Football Conference.

From the moment they left the field in Super Bowl XXV beaten by the narrowest of margins, the Bills became obsessed with one objective—to get back. All year long they had pointed to this date—January 26, 1992, and place—the Metrodome in Minneapolis. They seemed to know the date as well as their own birthdates and anniversaries. And they now knew they would be facing an excellent Redskins team that had lost only two games and demolished the Detroit Lions 41–10 for the NFC crown.

Although Washington may have lacked the star power of the Bills, the Redskins had quality players all over the field and they played in the tough NFC East. Additionally, it could not be forgotten, the NFC had won the last seven Super Bowls. Redskins quarterback Mark Rypien had been sacked only seven times all season, and he had two game-breaking receivers in Art Monk and Gary Clark. Washington also had a strong running game, powered by Earnest Byner and Gerald Riggs and the agile Ricky Ervins. And Wilber Marshall was a force on defense who could take over a game. Perhaps the most celebrated component of Washington was its massive offensive line, appropriately and affectionately called "the Hogs."

There was a misconception that Washington was a running team since the Redskins had not played a game all year under a dome. Playing indoors, it was thought, would give the Bills fast-break offense a big advantage on a fast track. Furthermore, the Bills believed their previous Super Bowl experience could only work to their benefit. There would be no distractions this time. They would be used to all the attention and would know how to handle the situation. "Maybe last year, we were just excited to be there," Bennett told the media.

"We might have had a little too much fun last year," Kelly agreed. "That's why we're approaching it differently this year. Last year was our first time, and we were in awe of everything."

"We're here with a mission this time," Keith McKeller said. "We don't want to just be in the Super Bowl. We want to *win* the Super Bowl."

Although he kept his feelings to himself in the days leading up to the game, Bill Polian was worried that his team had already expended everything it had to get back to the Super Bowl. It was going to take a herculean effort to turn back a Redskins team that had dominated the NFC throughout the season. "You could argue that we really didn't belong there," Polian said years later. "We were so beaten and battered. Ray Bentley playing on one arm, Shane Conlan and Bruce Smith playing on one leg. That was a miracle season to get there. Washington was by far the better team."

But Buffalo's fans were convinced this was their time. The caravan started with Ralph Wilson, who would bring the entire Bills family to the game. "Every one of those Super Bowls we went to, he took every single person in the organization," Levy said. "He had them flown down, meals, tickets. I'm talking about the ladies who cleaned up at night, switchboard operators, everybody. There was very high morale there. And the fan base was such in Buffalo. Yes, there's [NHL] hockey, but there's no Major League Baseball, no NBA basketball, no really major college football close by. So the focus was heavily on the Bills."

It was only the second Super Bowl held in a cold-weather city and the Buffalonians felt right at home. Fans poured into Minneapolis from Rochester, New York, and Erie, Pennsylvania, and Toronto, Canada, in their vintage red, white, and blue Bills regalia. And nearly all of them, it seemed, tried to make their way into the Radisson Hotel in downtown St. Paul, overlooking the Mississippi River, where the team was staying. "The Buffalo people just overwhelmed the hotels and restaurants," Dennis DiPaolo said. "Everyone just loved the Bills. The people spent their money. The Bills always put my family up at the hotel with the team, and when I got there I walked into the lobby and there was a small little bar, and I asked if the manager was around since we were in the restaurant business. And he came over, and I told him in the next few days, this place was going to be overwhelmed with Buffalo people, and my advice would be to set up as many small bars as can be. And that first night when the fans started to come in, they were just overwhelmed. And the next day I saw the manager running around, and he had garbage cans filled with beer. We enjoyed our team and we enjoyed every moment they provided for us. We loved traveling with them."

Donn Bartz, who has lived in Buffalo since 1935, remembered, "all week long they're saying how hard the Bills are practicing and bearing down for this game. Meanwhile, the Redskins practice and then go out ice fishing and enjoy themselves and they were just loose. And I thought the Bills were actually too tense, too intent on trying to win this. I think if you play loose, you'll have a better chance of winning."

Kelly tried to put on an easygoing game face and spin on the challenge: "Not that many teams get a second opportunity. This is every player's dream since he was a little boy, might as well enjoy it. I just happen to be one of the two quarterbacks here this year. Now it's a matter of us going out and capitalizing on it."

Steve Tasker, the Bills superb special teams player, was cautious in his assessment. "We'll have to play extremely well to beat them," he said. "You have to give Washington a little bit of an edge. They're a well-rounded team. They're going to be tough to stop."

Thomas had not said much during the week leading up to the game. He skipped his media session appointment, later saying, "I understood I was scheduled to go on at 8:30. It was 8:45, and nobody had come to get me. I got upset. I went back to my room." The coach and the quarterback were slated to be the featured speakers in a separate room, beginning at 8:30 that morning. All the other Bills, including the reigning MVP of the league, were to meet in a nearby conference room a half hour later. It was not the grand stage Thomas had envisioned for himself.

Not even being named the league's Most Valuable Player could mollify what he considered a perceived slight. "Even though I did get the MVP of the league, some still call me the No. 3 running back behind Barry Sanders or Emmitt Smith," he said.

"Look how long it's taken for me to get recognition," Thomas said in Minneapolis that week. "I don't understand that. I don't know whether it's the small market of Buffalo, or whether we've got celebrities on the team like Kelly and Andre Reed and Bruce Smith. It's some of the interviews I don't receive. I'm still not known everywhere, just in Buffalo. I don't think many people know me in Los Angeles. The only reason they know me in Houston is because I'm from there. It should be where even if I had a bad year, the media would still want to talk to me."

The game began on an ominous note for Buffalo. Thomas could not find his helmet and was not on the field for the Bills' first two plays. The running back had a pregame ritual in which he would place his helmet on the 34-yard line, but his helmet was moved when the stage was constructed for Harry Connick Jr. to sing the national anthem.

As it turned out, Thomas and the Bills never got going. Three times in the game's early minutes during the scoreless first quarter, Washington moved into Buffalo's red zone, only to finally come away with a single field goal early in the second quarter. That was positioned by Rypien's 41-yard connection with his wide receiver Ricky Sanders despite blitz pressure from the Bills. It was also a sign of things to come. The Washington quarterback quickly took control of the game.

On their next series with the Bills defense backing up to seal the deep routes, Rypien went to his short passing game: 16 yards to Clark, eight more to Monk, and on second-and-9 at the 10, he found Byner for the game's first touchdown.

With their next possession, Washington employed three tight ends, and Rypien managed to find Clark down the middle for 34 yards to set up Riggs' 1-yard touchdown run. Suddenly it was 17–0 Redskins.

The Bills were stunned. It was as if the Metrodome roof were falling down on them. Certainly no one could blame Don Beebe, the Bills wide receiver, for feeling that way. Late in the first half, Beebe had his hands on a pass near the goal line, but he was drilled by the safety, Brad Edwards, and the ball fell to the turf.

To compound their failure, two plays later Reed argued in vain with an official that he had been interfered with on his route. Not getting the call, he slammed his helmet to the ground and received a 15-yard unsportsmanlike conduct penalty. That infraction moved the ball from the Redskins 28-yard line back to the 43 and out of field-goal range. "It was a frustrating point in the game," a disconsolate Kelly later said. "There were many of those, though."

"If we had been at the top of our game from a confidence standpoint, we should have been able to pick them apart," Beebe still believes. "I'll agree we were a battered team, but everybody was healthy enough to at least play the game. It was my worst game I ever played."

It was Beebe's first Super Bowl—he had been sidelined the year before against the Giants—and now he was overcome by the occasion. "I got caught up in the emotion and making sure that my family and friends were all taken care of with tickets and hotel rooms and then realizing, *Oh, crap, there's a game,*" he said. "It just wasn't my mentally sharpest game. And I can probably speak for about everybody that was in that game. It was just ugly. We had six turnovers."

"We went into that game, knowing we'd have to play a great game to beat them, and we didn't," Pete Metzelaars said. "It was just self-inflicted pressure, I guess, trying to prove to everybody we can win this thing. We deserve to be here. We should be here… Because of that pressure we put on ourselves, instead of just going out and playing free and relaxed, the pressure kind of built, built, built."

On the other side of the ball, Rypien was having the game of his life. Buffalo thought they could get to him, rattle him, knock him down, with Smith and Bennett supplying the pressure. Indeed they did hit Rypien a good half dozen times, but the quarterback stood his ground and managed to find his receivers. He was never sacked.

Trailing 17–0 at halftime, there was talk in the Buffalo locker room of making the greatest comeback in Super Bowl history. But the only people who really held out that kind of hope were the Bills themselves. James Lofton remembers walking out to the field before the start of the game and seeing boxes with Super Bowl champion hats for Buffalo stacked against the wall of the tunnel. However, when the Bills headed back to the field after the half-time break, Lofton noticed that all the boxes were gone.

And any thoughts of a dramatic rally were quickly dismissed on the first play of the second half. Washington linebacker Andre Collins cut loose on a blitz right up the middle, and Kelly hurried his throw. Kurt Gouveia stepped in front of Keith McKeller and picked it off at the 25-yard line and returned it to the 2. Riggs quickly scored his second touchdown.

The Bills managed a modest comeback, slicing the deficit to 24–10 midway through the third quarter after a short field goal by Norwood and a 1-yard touchdown run by Thomas. But Washington then put the game out of reach with a long drive reminiscent of the Giants' punishing drives the year before. The Redskins went 79 yards in 11 plays; the finishing touch was Rypien's 30-yard touchdown pass to Clark near the end of the third quarter.

It was 31–10 and it could have been a lot worse. In the first half, the Redskins had an early touchdown called back and botched an easy field-goal attempt on the very next play. Not that it mattered. After Washington went up 37–10, the Bills scored a couple of inconsequential touchdowns to make the final score of 37–24. The final tally made the game appear much more competitive than it really was.

As the players headed to the locker room, an unlikely skirmish broke out on the field. "Jim Ritcher's son and my son got into a fight over why we lost the game," Metzelaars remembered years later, laughing. *"It was your dad's fault. No it was your dad's fault.* They were so upset over the fact that we lost the game. They were so disappointed. They were nine, 10 years old. Great friends, great buddies. They couldn't understand, *How did we lose again?*"

If the loss to the Giants had been devastating, this one was humiliating. Kelly threw four interceptions, was responsible for five turnovers, and was sacked five times. It hardly mattered that Thomas couldn't find his hat at the outset. He gained only 13 yards on 10 carries and was limited to 27 yards on four receptions.

Rypien was named the game's MVP. He had the kind of day Kelly had often dreamed about as a young boy. Rypien completed 18-of-33 passes for 292 yards and two touchdowns. He became the third Redskins quarterback to win a Super Bowl under Joe Gibbs' tutelage.

It was a painful loss, especially for Kelly, who had briefly left the game in the fourth quarter after he had suffered a blow to the head scrambling for a first down. He missed only one play, feeling "kind of fuzzy." Afterward, team doctors told him he had suffered a concussion. "I wanted to win a Super Bowl," Kelly said sadly. "Terry Bradshaw is my idol, Joe Namath. I guess it wasn't supposed to be. I just didn't do it tonight."

Buffalo's big-play passing attack never materialized. Playing from behind, way behind, Kelly attempted a Super Bowl–record 58 passes, a hollow testament underscored by the measly 4.7 yards gained per pass attempt. Although he completed 28 passes, Lofton's longest catch was for 18 yards, and Reed's best went for just 12 yards. To make matters worse, the Buffalo team that led the league in rushing, ran just 18 times against Washington and gained a paltry 43 yards.

"They didn't use me enough," Thomas complained in the aftermath. "I don't know what the coaches were thinking. You just can't get away from the running game. That's what got us here.

I felt I should have been used more in the first half. Their defense jammed the middle. I felt we could have run the ball on the outside and we would have had a better chance at winning the game. We made a lot of mistakes and we didn't adjust to some of the things that they were doing." Thomas seemed to be in denial of what Washington had done to him. They had stacked five and six men at the line of scrimmage, ensuring Buffalo would not run on them.

"We didn't make the plays we usually make," Kelly said, fumbling for answers. "We just got outplayed. They brought a lot of people, and we missed some chances against them. I held the ball a little too long a couple of times. We missed a couple of blocks, and there were a couple of drops."

It seemed fairly evident that everything that could go wrong had gone wrong. Smith could not believe what had transpired. "To be honest, I'm still in dismay," he told reporters. "I still can't believe this. It hurts, but it still hasn't hit me fully. When it does, it's gonna hit me hard. I can't say I'm not going to think about it. That would be a lie. We're gonna think about it a long time."

The year had ended on a sour note yet again. The Bills could build on their loss to the Giants in the Super Bowl. They had played with poise and displayed great character in competing right to the very end in Tampa. But in Minneapolis, they played poorly and they knew it. And they knew the Redskins were not just better than them on this given Sunday, they were a clearly superior champion. "We've got the talent to win Super Bowls, but we just can't do it," Thomas said. Then he invoked another perennial AFC power that had come up short in the biggest game four times: "We're falling into the category of the Denver Broncos."

A few admitted they had been fearful of losing during the week leading up to the game, fully aware that the victorious team from the NFC had lifted the Lombardi Trophy the previous seven years. "We talked about losing before the game," cornerback Kirby Jackson confessed. "We wanted to end that streak. We didn't want to come in here and lose two Super Bowls. We didn't want to be known as the team that goes to the Super Bowl and loses. Now we have to keep fighting to get back here and win one."

At least he was willing to carry the good fight forward another year. The same could not be said, in the moments following this momentous loss, for Thomas, who sounded off with a bitter fury. "I want to play for someone else," Thomas was ranting late into the Minneapolis night. "I truly want the hell out of Buffalo. It's not the people of Buffalo. It's the organization. There's a lot of personal stuff. For me to get up and say this or that, I can't get into it now. I just want out."

One bad game and suddenly it was Armageddon. But just as Thomas was inconspicuous in this Super Bowl, no one paid much attention to what he was saying afterward.

"You get a W or an L," Darryl Talley said. "Now I have two damn L's." But Talley was more measured with his words, already employing his leadership skills. "We had 47 players and a coaching staff here," he continued. "We were all in this together. We're not going to start pointing fingers at each other. We lost as a team." Deep down he knew one loss, even another loss in the Super Bowl, was not the end of the world. "All I'll think about for the next six months is this game," Talley said.

"When you lose a Super Bowl you have some doubts," Wright, the nose tackle, remembered years later, from his time in the trenches. "When you lose a second Super Bowl, you really have doubts. But we had a special character on that team. We had a lot of guys who were mortar between the bricks. We had lot of superstars on the team. Eight guys would go to the Pro Bowl every year. They were the glue."

And they were the ones who would have to hold the team together if they were to make another run, one more time, to a third straight Super Bowl. "We may fall every now and then," Thomas was finally able to say. "We always get up."

And so they would.

CHAPTER 9 | A Testament to Buffalo's Resiliency

THE PROSPECT OF a third straight trip to the Super Bowl seemed to diminish significantly in a late December 1992 game in New Orleans when Bruce Smith, Cornelius Bennett, Shane Conlan, and Kirby Jackson, the foundation of their defense, were all injured. Although the Bills managed to win their 11th game of the season that day, 20–16 over the New Orleans Saints, the plane ride home was long and hardly festive. The Bills knew they had to go back on the road the next week and beat a Houston Oilers team headed for the playoffs if they were to secure home-field advantage throughout the postseason.

As it turned out with their depleted defense already reeling in Houston, the Bills suffered yet another crippling blow in the second quarter. Trailing 10–3, Jim Kelly suffered what Buffalo feared was a season-ending injury. The Oilers went on to drill the Bills 27–3, setting up an instant rematch the following weekend in the wild-card match.

On a rainy, windy Saturday in Buffalo, it appeared the Bills' Super Bowl bid was coming to an abrupt end. Kelly and Bennett were not in uniform and could only watch an awesome first-half performance by Warren Moon, who threw for four touchdowns as the Oilers exploded to a 28–3 halftime lead.

The game was all but over. The thousands of fans who were streaming out of Rich Stadium during the intermission knew it was over. Even the Bills knew it. They weren't kidding themselves. "We got our tails whipped the week before, down in Houston," Beebe remembered. "That had to be in your mind-set, going through the week in practice. And then we come out and just played terrible and we're down 28–3 at halftime. And I remember my locker's next to Steve Tasker's, and he's got this sense of humor about him. He always has these one-liners, king of one-liners. He says, 'Well, Beebs, where are we golfing next week?'"

Darryl Talley wasn't laughing. And he wasn't about to call it a day either. "I was screaming at everybody in the locker room, telling them, 'If you quit, I'm coming after you. We're going to fight back and win this thing.' And guys are looking at me like I'd lost my mind," Talley said.

To his teammates he looked like a man possessed, demonized. He was screaming about hitting Oilers if they're five yards out of bounds. He was screaming about putting a hurt on Houston, so they wouldn't be able to play the next week if they happened to win. He seemed to be making little sense. He was clearly crossing the lines of fair play. But he was inspiring.

The coach believed in him. Levy looked at his troops and calmly reminded his men that they had won the last two AFC crowns. "Hey, you're two-time defending champions. When you walk off the field, don't let anyone ever say you quit."

Gale Gilbert, the third-string quarterback, reminded Reich, now piloting the team in Kelly's absence, of a famous comeback he had engineered at Maryland. "You did this in college," Gilbert told him. "No reason you can't do it here."

"In college it took one play at a time," Reich recalls of that day. In 1984 his Maryland team was losing to defending-national-champion Miami by 31–0 at halftime, before he brought them back to win 42–40. "In college the defense had to shut them down. In college it took the special teams to have to make a play. No one person does it. And that's what we talked about at halftime. You're not thinking, 'We're gonna go out and win.' You're thinking, 'We just gotta go out and take it one play at a time.' And that should be your attitude all the time. But there are certain times in a game and a season when you really end up honing in on the basics. Nobody wants to get embarrassed, period. Nobody wants to get embarrassed in the playoffs. And nobody wants to get embarrassed in the playoffs at home."

Don Beebe remembered, "Frank's not a yeller or a screamer like Darryl is. He's more methodical and deep-thinking, and Frank's way of motivating us is like, 'Okay they scored 28. Why can't we in the second half? Let's just start making plays one at a time.'"

When the second half began, Rich Stadium was half full or half empty, depending on how you look at things. "Halftime comes, and half the stadium leaves," Donn Bartz, a die-hard fan said. "And I don't care who you talk to, they'll tell you they were there. They weren't. We're sitting there, and the Oilers are knocking us all over the place. I have never left a game early. Our whole group is sitting there. And the Oilers come out and score right away, and we're down even more."

Reich's first pass of the second half was intercepted by Houston safety Bubba McDowell, who raced 58 yards into the end zone to make it 35–3. No NFL team had ever come back from such a deficit to win a playoff game.

"There's just got to be a mental fortitude of never say quit, never say die," Reich believes to this day. "You feel like you were trained that way as a player your whole life. I was trained that way by my mom and dad. It's not like when you're in the moment, 'I gotta make a decision whether I'm going to continue to play hard or not.' You do what you've been trained to do. You just do what comes naturally in those times."

Reich had been throwing passes his whole life, and staring down a 32-point margin, he began completing them in bunches. The Bills were on the move. Kenneth Davis scored from one yard out to bring them within four touchdowns. Then the Bills caught their first break. Steve Christie, who had replaced Scott Norwood during the offseason, recovered his own onside kick. To this day Levy insists it was a flub and not planned. Nevertheless, Reich quickly connected with Beebe for a 38-yard touchdown. Replays showed that Beebe stepped out of bounds before catching the ball, but the NFL had not yet instituted instant replay. At 35–17 it was beginning to feel like a ball game. With Talley leading the defensive charge, the Bills got the ball right back. Reich found Andre Reed for a 26-yard touchdown. The Oilers' lead was down to 35–24, and the stadium was in an uproar.

Fans who were listening to the game on the radio in the parking lots began to reenter the gates. The game had not been sold out, so television coverage was blacked out in Buffalo. Crafty locals had a get-around: you could drive across Lake Erie into Canada, where it was broadcast on Canadian TV. Fans who had watched in distant bars or listened on the radio at home began to gravitate toward the stadium. You could sense something historic was happening.

"Phones started to ring," an Allegeny, New York, fan said. "'You believe what's going on? You believe this?' And the word got out that they were starting to let people back into the stadium. So I headed there. I was 15 minutes away. People were like, *are you kidding me? Is this really happening?*"

The NFL had a security rule preventing fans from reentering the stadium once they had left, so dozens of them started to climb over a fence. Finally, the Bills security force relented and reopened the gates as a safety precaution. Anyone could walk in for free and sit anywhere. As the third quarter was winding down, the stadium was starting to fill up once again. It felt to many like crashing a party, like getting away with something.

The next time Moon got his hands on the ball he threw an interception. On fourth-and-5 from the 18-yard line, Reich again hit Reed in the end zone, cutting Houston's lead to 35–31. It was Reich's third touchdown pass in seven minutes. When he hooked up with Reed for their third touchdown, the Bills had their first lead, 38–35, with just over three minutes remaining. Rich Stadium was in a frenzy. Yet the Oilers were not finished. Moon drove them 63 yards in a dozen plays, and Al Del Greco hit a 26-yard field goal to force overtime.

When Houston won the toss to get the ball first in overtime, an unsettling feeling descended on the stadium. The Oilers had just driven down the field to tie the game. If they could get in position for one more field goal, the game would be theirs, and the Bills' great comeback would be all for naught. But Buffalo's defense came through. Nate Odomes intercepted Moon's pass, and three plays later, Christie's field goal ended the dramatic comeback once and for all time—41–38. "It was the ultimate 'it's not over till it's over' game," Tasker said.

Behind their backup quarterback, the Bills had staged an unforgettable comeback. "After the onside kick and we scored, it's 35–17. I thought, 'Uh, oh, this could happen,'" Reich said. "And certainly after the next touchdown, it got to be 35–24. That's when I felt it. *We're gonna win.* The fans were just going berserk. It was insane.

"One of the unique things about players is, you don't want to let your teammates down. Sure, I like playing well and being respected for that, but the personal [glory] was not what I was living for. I got more joy out of the being part of the team aspect of it—not only my immediate team and the coaches and the organization, but my family and the fans of Buffalo, seeing what it does to that whole family, to the city. To me, that's just exciting stuff."

It had been a surreal day from start to finish. Beebe still talks about "the tremendous euphoria at the beginning of the game with 80,000 people and then to experience 50,000 people because they all left. It looked empty. And then to see and hear it packed again, and by the ending of the game how loud it was. I never heard a stadium that loud. I literally was on the ground, and it felt like an earthquake. You could feel the ground moving almost. It was that loud in that stadium that day."

Under damp gray skies, the Bills shook down the thunder. Reich had brought them all the way back in the second half, and his calm demeanor proved to be the difference. He had convinced his teammates to take it one play at a time and assured them that they would find their comfort zone. With his words and actions, he put them at ease—and in position to win a lost game.

"Many players have experienced being in the zone," Beebe said. "It's one of those feelings where it almost feels like time has stopped. You're completely relaxed...It's like anything you do is going well. And that's what it felt like that day in the second half. Everything that we did was just easy. And it goes back to faith. Don't ever give up. Great things can happen.

"There's one word that wins. This is a secret," Beebe said with a laugh. "You've got to have this. It's called 'chemistry.' Forget talent. Throw talent out the window. All these teams have talent. If you don't have chemistry, you're not going to win. And what that means is you really have to care about the guy you're playing with, the coach that's coaching you, and really enjoy your time in practice and you'll get much better practices in. And when the game's on the line and you're down 35–3 against Houston, you're going to make a comeback. That's chemistry. And I think that's really what made up the core of the Bills' run."

For Talley the feeling was magical. He felt empowered that day. "That game made me believe we were really special," he said. "Everybody else in America was throwing the towel in on us, but we were looking at each other going, 'Okay, we're gonna do this and we're gonna come back and win this football game.'"

Indeed, they were beginning to feel like a team of destiny. "Absolutely," Reich said. "We'd already lost two Super Bowls, and this was it."

"Destiny? I didn't think in those terms," Levy said. "I'm thinking, 'Next week we go to Pittsburgh. Will our hurt guys be back? What's our plan?'"

"We were without a lot of our star players," Jim Ritcher remembered. "It was mostly determination. Most of our wins were because of star players like Kelly and Thurman and Bruce, and to come back and win showed we were a team."

"The Houston comeback reenergized us," Mark Kelso said. "That reinvigorated us. I thought there was no stopping us now. I felt we were destined to win."

Despite all the injuries, their confidence was high. They would somehow find a way to win three more games. Reich quarterbacked at Pittsburgh, handling a 24–3 win. Kelly returned in Miami, and the Bills prevailed 29–10 against a stalwart Dolphins team. Just like that the Bills were on their way to a third straight Super Bowl.

Three playoff games won. One to go.

CHAPTER 10 | Super Bowl XXVII

No matter how sophisticated the National Football League's scouting divisions have become and how informative its research departments are, it is not uncommon for a player to overcome great odds and take circuitous routes before making it to the big show.

Kurt Warner stocked supermarket shelves before his Super Bowl career flourished in St. Louis and Arizona. Warren Moon was undrafted coming out of the University of Washington and had to win five Grey Cup championships in Canada before the Houston Oilers gave him a chance in the NFL. Antonio Gates, the muscular tight end, had not played football since high school when the San Diego Chargers signed him.

And then there was Don Beebe, who traveled as unlikely a path as anyone could imagine in order to catch the attention of scouts from the NFL. A 5′10″ wide receiver with blinding speed, Beebe spent three years away from a football field, working in construction, hanging aluminum siding on houses, before he decided to go back to college and give the game one more shot.

But his road to the NFL was much longer than that. It began in 1983, when he started at Western Illinois University on a football scholarship. He barely made it through the fall of his freshman year because he was homesick and missed his girlfriend and ended up transferring to a junior college and played basketball. Then he quit school altogether and turned to construction. When he tried to return to Western Illinois, he was told he didn't have enough credits to transfer. By the time he had earned the requisite credits, his eligibility to play football had expired. Luckily Beebe got a reprieve under an obscure NCAA reentry rule. He went on to catch 29 passes for five touchdowns for the Leathernecks.

Concluding his college career, Beebe faced a difficult decision: apply for the 1988 NFL Draft and hope to get picked up in the late rounds or attend a smaller, NAIA school to beef up his résumé. Beebe chose Chadron State College in tiny Chadron, Nebraska. The rest is the stuff of fantasy. Beebe caught 49 passes at Chadron and, more important, the attention of NFL scouts.

"What happened was I ran a miraculous 40[-yard dash] time for a combine scout one day, and he said, 'I got to get you into the Combine,'" he remembered. The Combine is the NFL's dog-and-pony show where football players run sprints and do agility drills in an effort to determine who has the right stuff to make it on the playing field. "So I get invited to this thing and I go in there and I break the all-time record for the 40-yard dash in a floppy Asics running fishing shoe. I didn't know I needed an agent and I didn't know I needed track shoes. I just showed up and ran a 4.25, and that record stood for 17 years until Chris Johnson broke it in 2007. So that had to happen. If I go in there and run a 4.45, I'm just another guy from Chadron who's never going to get drafted."

Beebe's vertical jump was also several inches higher than average, and his long jump exceeded the norm. Suddenly the kid had the attention of all 28 NFL teams. "So after that workout—Bill

Polian will tell you till this day it's still the best combine workout he's ever witnessed—I had 21 personal workouts for the next two months." Beebe continued. "Every day it seemed like I was working out for somebody, running the 40 and catching balls because they couldn't believe it. So many teams were serious, I knew I was going to go anywhere from the second to the fourth round."

Polian nabbed him in the third round. Beebe was the 82nd pick in the 1989 draft. With his sprinter's speed, he quickly became a fan favorite in Buffalo when he raced away from a Houston Oilers defensive back in this third professional game for a 63-yard touchdown reception. The Houston defender was left clutching only the middle E from Beebe's torn jersey as the fleet receiver reached the end zone. For the rest of the game BE BE shined. A Buffalo radio station even playfully initiated a search for the missing E.

As he entered his fourth season in 1992, he was coming off his best year, 32 receptions and six touchdowns. And just as it had been in his first three seasons in Buffalo, the expectations were high for the Bills. "From Year One it was, 'Yeah, we're going to the Super Bowl,'" Beebe said. "I don't ever remember in the offseason and early in the season that guys were not talking about the Super Bowl. It was almost like a given that we're going. I don't ever remember a time when we weren't going."

No less a die-hard fan than Buffalo native Tim Russert invoked a prayer for his Bills as he ended his broadcast of *Meet the Press* on Super Bowl Sunday morning, January 31, 1993. "Now it's in God's hands," Russert said, smiling. "God is good. God is just. Please, God, make three a charm. Our time has come." Then, raising his right thumb up, Russert said hopefully, "Our time has come."

It would be no small task. The Bills were coming up against a young team that was determined to restore luster to a franchise with a proud history that had recently fallen on hard times. These new-and-improved Dallas Cowboys had arrived on the scene in a hurry with a freewheeling coach in Jimmy Johnson and three emerging megawatt stars on offense in Troy Aikman, Emmitt Smith, and Michael Irvin.

There was a swagger about Johnson, a cockiness that set him apart from other NFL coaches. He arrived in Pasadena for his first Super Bowl, brimming with confidence bordering on arrogance, certain his Cowboys had cleared their biggest hurdle by overcoming the 49ers 30–20 in the mud of Candlestick Park. "We thought San Francisco was probably the best team in the league and once we won that game felt like we were pretty well in good shape," Johnson told reporters. He was so relaxed on Super Bowl Sunday that he went out for a jog on the morning of the game.

"I really didn't have a lot of concerns," he said years later. "I don't think I've ever gone into any game where I felt as confident that we were gonna win. If I had any concerns at all, it would've been their no-huddle offense. But we had two weeks to get ready for it, and what I did to prepare for it was, I had all of our offensive players break up into two units and we ran one play right after another. Of course, they're running off cards, so we were able to machine gun the plays toward the defense. But we really didn't have a lot of concerns because we knew Buffalo turned the ball over a lot and we didn't. And we figured that was gonna be the difference in the ballgame."

But it was Dallas who suffered the first miscue in Super Bowl XXVII. Steve Tasker blocked a first-quarter Dallas punt, and a few plays later Thurman Thomas, battling shoulder and ankle injuries, rumbled into the end zone. Suddenly the Bills had a 7–0 lead. "Oh, they blocked a punt," Johnson remembered dismissively.

"We had an injury before the game and we lost our four-five punt protectors, and I had to put a young linebacker in his spot. And they ended up blocking the punt to start the ballgame, and that kind of put us in a hole. We were confident that eventually they would turn the ball over, and that was gonna be the game. We were confident they were gonna turn it over—an interception, one thing or another."

However unorthodox it may sound, it turned out to be the right a game plan. That 7–0 lead quickly dissolved as Buffalo's center Kent Hull was injured, and Kelly began to collapse under the relentless pressure of the Cowboys pass rushers. First, he threw an interception that Aikman quickly converted into a touchdown. Then, a few seconds later, Charles Haley spun around Howard Ballard and sacked Kelly at the 2-yard line and forced a fumble. Jimmie Jones picked up the loose ball and ran in for the score. The Cowboys' two touchdowns came only 15 seconds apart, a new Super Bowl record.

On their first series of the second quarter, Kelly hit Andre Reed for 40 yards, down to the Dallas 4. On fourth-and-goal from the 1, the Bills decided to go for a touchdown and Dallas substituted, taking out two goal-line defenders, crowding the passing lanes. Kelly rolled to his right looking first for Thomas and then tried to lob it to Carwell Gardner deep in the end zone. Dallas safety Thomas Everett cut in front of the fullback for the interception.

It was Kelly's third turnover. And Marv Levy took the blame. "I should have called timeout," he said later. "We had a play called but not for that defense."

The next time the Bills got the ball, still trailing 14–7, Ken Norton, the Cowboys linebacker and son of the former heavyweight boxing champion, came on a furious blitz and, as he was blocked, crashed into Kelly's right knee. The quarterback collapsed in agony. He had missed the first two playoff games with sprained ligaments in his right knee and he had sprained them again. He was done for the day.

Frank Reich stepped in and, as he had four weeks before against Houston, immediately connected with Reed for 38 yards to set up a short field goal by Steve Christie that made it 14–10. But then the Cowboys cut the heart out of the Bills. Aikman and Irvin hooked up for touchdown passes of 19 and 18 yards around a Thomas fumble with Irvin dunking the pigskin over the goal post in celebration. His two touchdowns took place within a span of 18 seconds in the final two minutes of the first half, propelling Dallas to a 28–10 halftime lead—thunderbolts that shook the Rose Bowl. The Bills looked shell-shocked as they headed to the locker room.

For a fleeting moment at the end of the third quarter, it appeared Buffalo might stage another big comeback. Beebe caught a 40-yard touchdown pass from Reich to narrow the deficit to 31–17. "I remember scoring the touchdown and kneeling down and praying and walking over to the sideline, 'We're only 14 points down. All right, it's still the third quarter. Let's just do this." Beebe remembered. "But I don't think everybody had that attitude. I just don't. I think there are just some guys—not that they quit, quitting is not the word, but emotionally just didn't have that edge. You've got to have that edge. That aura and moxie about you, that pep in the step that [makes you feel] you're going to make the play. And we just couldn't finish it."

The Bills were finished early in the fourth quarter when Aikman threw a 45-yard touchdown pass to Alvin Harper. The rout was on. Supported by crutches on the sidelines, Kelly was heard to mutter, "What did I ever do to deserve this?"

Darryl Talley couldn't begin to find the words to try and rally his teammates. "We limped into the Super Bowl and physically we were shredded," he said years later. "Nobody was healthy. Nobody was productive. We ran into a buzz saw that day. That game there, that was one we took on the chin."

They unraveled on the biggest stage in sports. They were hurt and embarrassed. "I know that I was bummed out," Kelly recalled. "We thought we could win every single game we played in. We're all pumped up. I know that maybe I pressed a little bit, threw interceptions that weren't very good. You try and you stay focused…" Kelly's voice trails off like an errant spiral.

Watching this horror show unfold, Polian was devastated. "It wasn't the defeat that was so bothersome," he said. "It was the fact that this great team, this great group of individuals, this unique incredible bunch who had overcome so much—even in that particular season with Frank playing all those games, the miracle comeback, the greatest comeback ever—was just being beaten to a pulp by another club. And I remember remarking to one of the staff people I was sitting with, 'Boy this is hard to watch, to see this happen to such a great group of guys.'" Years later, Polian chokes back emotion and strains to say, "And that's my thought even today."

The Bills were beaten to a pulp, but the game was far from over. Reich was still trying to move the Bills, determined to get one last touchdown when he was sacked and fumbled, and Leon Lett scooped up the ball and began running for the end zone 65 yards away.

Beebe was running, too, a fly pattern way down the sideline, just as he had hundreds, even thousands of times before. Beebe said, "And the next thing I see is a Dallas Cowboy pick the football up. I didn't care who it was. He picked it up, he started to run.

Well, I took off right away. I just reacted in a split second. It was my character. It was who I was being revealed at that point in time in that football game. Forget about football, this could happen in life. How you react to something is your true character. So I just started running."

As Lett, an enormous man at 6'6" and 290 pounds, got near the end zone he tried to emulate his flamboyant teammate Irvin, who had already scored two touchdowns that day and showboated in the end zone. Lett laid the ball out in his right hand, palming the ball for all the world to see, as Beebe with his sprinter's speed, ran him down. "I just knocked the ball out just inside the 1-yard line," Beebe said. "If I had thought about it for just a second, I'd never have made the play. I just took off."

The ball rolled out of bounds for a touchback. Beebe had run nearly the length of the field to deny the Cowboys one more score in a 52–17 blowout. There would be no more showboating on his watch. "That tells you all you need to know about the Buffalo Bills," Polian proudly said. "That tells you what that team was about. That's the heart of the story and that's the heart of the team. Adversity's an opportunity for heroism. Well, Beebe believed it, thankfully—right down to the last moment."

Beebe walked off the field that night no less disgusted and dejected than any of his teammates. They had been humiliated and turned the ball over an embarrassing nine times. None of them wanted to talk to anyone. Beebe went straight to his locker, slumped down, and leaned over with his elbows on his knees, his hands cradling his sweaty face.

"The next thing I know the owner walks in, Ralph Wilson. And I'm kind of in the quarterback area where Frank and Jim were, and Mr. Wilson went for a beeline right over to me," Beebe said. "And he had a point of what he wanted to say. There's no question about that. He put his hand on my shoulder. It's a sign of gratitude when somebody puts a hand on you, and he said to me—he didn't call me Don or No. 82—he said, 'Son, you showed me a lot tonight. Just thank you so much for showing everybody in this country what Buffalo is all about, what the Bills are all about.' When he said that, it kind of hit home. As dejected as I was, 'Wow, that meant a lot to him.'"

Beebe soon found out how much that great chase meant to so many more. They wanted him in the interview room. The media wanted to know why he would run Lett down. "You're done. Let him go," Beebe remembers them saying. "I said, 'No, you don't understand. That's not the way I was brought up.'"

It was the signature moment for a team that had fought back year after year just to get to the Super Bowl. One player giving everything he had in a hopeless cause because there was still time on the clock, still work to be done. And it resonated with millions of Americans. It wasn't about talent, it was about desire. It was the kind of play every man could relate to. "That's true," Beebe says. "It's not like you're out there throwing six touchdowns. And that's me. I was a construction guy. I'm every guy's living dream, every guy that pounds nails wants to play in the Super Bowl."

When he got back home to Buffalo, box loads of fan mail began arriving almost daily. A hundred or more letters poured in each day for several weeks from all around the country. They were from parents and coaches, and especially from fathers thanking Beebe for showing their sons how to play the game to the bitter end with everything you've got.

A couple of months later, *Sports Illustrated* reached out to Beebe and Lett and asked them to meet with each other to talk about the play. That's how big it got. It was a favorite topic on talk radio and in the newspapers. So the two players who did not know each other met in a bagel shop in West Palm Beach, Florida, not far from where Beebe was staying. Beebe arrived early, as is his custom, and was seated when Lett entered. "In walked this huge man through the threshold of the doors," Beebe said, "and I got out of my chair and introduced myself. I said, 'Leon, I agreed to do this as long as there'd be no physical abuse.' That kind of broke the ice. So we had about 10 minutes before the sports reporter got there, and I got to find out that this was a great guy, really a gentle giant of a man. Quiet spirit about him. Not braggadocios at all. That's not how he came off. I really liked Leon."

When Austin Murphy of *Sports Illustrated* arrived and began the interview, he asked each man the same opening question: how has your life changed since the Super Bowl? Beebe went first. "Well, I'll be honest with you," he said. "It's been overwhelming. It's been tremendous, the response."

Then it was Lett's turn. And, as Beebe recalls, he was stunned by his answer. "Leon goes, 'Well, Mr. Murphy, to be honest, I'm afraid to go down the driveway to get my mail. I get hate mail and racial mail and death threats almost every day.' I'm thinking, 'Holy smokes, you've got to be kidding me.' On one side I'm almost feeling sorry for him and on the other I'm thinking all you had to do was finish, run as fast as you can, and I never would have caught you.

"And it's one of the stories I like to tell people," Beebe said recently. "It's that if you finish—I don't care what you lose or what you don't gain—if you give it everything you've got, you can live with the result. Every time. And the irony is if Leon would have given it everything in his power to try and score that touchdown, and Don Beebe still knocked that ball out of his hands and out of the back of the back of the end zone, nobody would have said one thing to Leon. Not one thing."

People still come up to Beebe years later, in airports or restaurants, and ask him about the Leon Lett play. That's how it's remembered: the Leon Lett Play. And Beebe himself still draws inspiration from it. "They go, 'You're that guy. Oh my God, I remember that play,'" Beebe said. "And I tell people that no matter what you do in life, if you just wake up in the morning with a good attitude and look at things as half-full and just keep plugging away no matter how hard it gets, you can always live with whatever happens to you. I don't care if it's a death in the family or bankruptcy or divorce, you've just got to keep plugging away. But the ones that don't—and sadly enough way too many people think the other way—that it's just going to be a miserable life. "And that play has brought so much notoriety and so much opportunity for me to publicly speak because I never should have played in the NFL. There's just no way. It's just a miracle from God that I played in the NFL."

CHAPTER 11 | A Cowboys Rematch

A**S THE TEAM** bus slowly drove out of Pasadena that evening, after one of the worst blowouts in Super Bowl history, Marv Levy and Bill Polian sat next to each other, commiserating like a beat-up old prizefighter and his trainer trying to figure out where it all went wrong. "Hurt isn't the word for it," Polian recalled. "Wounded beyond recognition is more like it."

The coach was more shocked than distraught by his team's inept performance. Throughout the season the Bills had won the turnover battle, but in the Rose Bowl that afternoon they looked like a bad college team that had been taken to the woodshed by the quicksilver Cowboys. "The nine turnovers worry you," Levy remembers. "You can't predict anything. We had been a positive giveaway-takeaway team all year long and now this. It was very painful."

As the bus headed toward team hotel, the coach continued to ruminate about the game with his general manager, echoing years past. "What should we have done differently?" Levy wondered about his mounting Super Bowl failures. "What should we have done differently in preparing?"

Polian turned a deaf ear and simply replied, "Marv, the only thing that really counts is what you do after the ball's kicked off. Don't overscrutinize what we ought to do differently. We didn't play well. We turned it over nine times. We didn't win."

The very same thoughts were running through the minds of so many players on the bus. A few guys had been crying in the locker room—a ghastly, almost inconceivable sight at the professional level. Some of them truly were in shock from the beating they had suffered. This was worse, much worse, than anything they had ever experienced on a football field, much worse even than the two previous Super Bowl losses.

Thurman Thomas tried to make some sense of it. "I don't know if we've been outcoached," he told the media after the game. "It seems like we have a good game plan going in, but once the game starts, things go wrong and we can't execute it."

Of the nine turnovers committed by the Bills, five led to Dallas touchdowns. Thomas couldn't bear to consider the math. Five touchdowns, 35 points: the margin of defeat. "We lost on the Norwood field goal and that hurt," Thomas said. "But this was embarrassing. This is not the way you want to end your season. If we had lost 38–37, that would have been bad. But you don't want to lose 52–17."

Steve Tasker was nearly at a loss for words. "The unbelievable thing is that each year it keeps getting worse, and I have no idea why," he said.

As the games would unwind and the Bills would unravel, Darryl Talley would try to cast aside any negative thoughts, put any notion of trepidation out of his mind. But he could not keep himself from second-guessing. "Why didn't I do this?" he still wonders. "Why didn't this work? Why couldn't we get it done? It eats at you."

Even after a crippling, humiliating loss, the veteran leadership had already resolved to put their nightmare in Pasadena behind them. On the flight from California back to Buffalo, Don Beebe and his teammates began talking defiantly of returning to the Super Bowl the next year. "There was no taking a month off or feeling sorry for yourself, no 'Gosh I hope we can get back,'" Beebe said. "It was, 'Guys we're going back. We're going to win this thing next year.' And that's all the talk you heard. I was so competitive, along with so many other guys on that football team, that we were just bound and determined to win that stupid game."

When they touched down in Buffalo, legions of their fans were assembled. By then, the Bills were already vowing revenge should the Cowboys make it back to the next Super Bowl. No matter which team they would face, they were determined to gain redemption for their own nervous breakdowns in the big game.

Jim Kelly was already sounding the battle cry: "Let's piss everybody off. Let's go back again." The Bills didn't need anyone to remind them they weren't "America's Team." Or that they couldn't win the big one. They had been to the big dance three consecutive times and went home brokenhearted each time. In the eyes of many, they had overstayed their welcome.

With each defeat Pete Metzelaars could feel that "the pressure mounted." To a man they tried to combat so much anxiety, but they had committed an astounding 14 turnovers in their last two Super Bowls. Clearly the burden to win was having a domino effect on players. "I don't know that we felt that or really believed that, but there's a little bit of 'Here we go again,'" Metzelaars said.

"When things are 'unraveling,' your mind-set is not *Uh, oh,* your mind-set is *just play ball,*" Frank Reich said. "You just got to focus on one play at a time. Did we get tight? That varies by the individual. Part of it is how the leaders on the team respond to that and the coach responds to that."

Even the coach had a hard time combating the sense of dread that was obviously engulfing his team on the field. Levy said, "You've got to correct things even while they're happening out there, where early in the game you go, 'Well, we've lost it.' You may have fallen behind. What changes do we need to make? Certainly if part of our game plan doesn't apply, let's abandon it. Let's speed it up. Let's slow it down. What are the tactics you're going to apply? You don't agonize during the game. And there are times you say, 'Oh darn it, and it's not over yet.'"

And still nothing works.

The Super Bowl is a game unlike any other in American sports. It's nothing short of a worldwide spectacle. It has become a de facto American holiday where people gather together and put on elaborate parties. It is played on our biggest stage with more than a hundred million Americans watching on TV and millions more around the world. Every play is magnified by such a huge lens. Every great play glorified. Every misstep examined and scrutinized. And the hardest obstacle to overcome should be the simplest objective to achieve: just play your game, play within yourself.

"Your emotions can get so high, so fast, in the game itself," Beebe said. "'I just scored a touchdown. I just made a great play. It's the Super Bowl.' You start thinking, *There are a billion people watching, and I just made this great play.* 'Okay, dude, you got to forget about it.' And then the reverse factor can happen. 'I just dropped a ball. I just missed a block, and Kelly got killed. I can't make a play. Everything's just in disarray. The game is so fast I can't see where they're coming from blitzing-wise, and we're missing our sight adjust routes and defensively we're just a step behind.' And so when that happens, your emotions can get very low, very fast."

And while Beebe's pursuit of Leon Lett at the end of an already lost game gained the admiration of sports fans, it also served as an inspiration for his teammates. It was the springboard, Levy said, to reach what he was calling "the impossible dream"—a fourth straight trip to the Super Bowl. The only question was whether the players had the drive and determination to fight back from such a staggering loss, if they had enough of what the coach calls character. "We weren't cursed," Darryl Talley says. "But you've got to be willing to endure all the pain and hard work that goes into getting back to the Super Bowl. You've got to really want it, and everybody on your team has to really want it just as bad because you know every team you go up against is going to be gunning for you."

Unfortunately Polian would not be with his players for another Super Bowl run. Four days later, he stunned all of Buffalo when he announced his departure from the organization. He was at odds with Jeff Littmann—the team's treasurer who also managed Ralph Wilson's business operation in Detroit—and their relationship had grown so contentious that Polian felt "it got to the point where it wasn't working." The architect of the Bills' rise to power was headed down the New York State Thruway to take a job at the NFL's headquarters in New York City, where he would counsel teams on the new free-agency plan.

To make matters worse, the schedule makers in the league seemed to have it out for the Bills, too. Because of the way the schedule rotates each season, each division facing off against each of the teams from another division, the Bills' were set to play the entire NFC East in 1993. It was a bitter irony. On the road, perhaps, to another Super Bowl, they would face off in the regular season against each of the three teams that had beaten them in the Super Bowl.

Then again, maybe it added some fuel to their fire. The Bills met the Dallas Cowboys, New York Giants, and Washington Redskins in the first seven weeks of the season, and they beat all three. None more contentious than the rematch of the Super Bowl rivals.

By the time the Bills traveled to Dallas to meet the Cowboys in the second week of the season, Emmitt Smith was two months into his contractual holdout with Jerry Jones. The Cowboys running back, the backbone of their attack, had been the NFL's leading rusher the previous two seasons and wanted to be compensated accordingly. He wanted to be paid more than Thomas, who was pulling down more than $13 million over four years. But the owner was unwilling to pay more than $11 million for four years.

As the teams took the field under a sweltering sky that turned Texas Stadium into an inferno with temperatures on the field approaching 110 degrees, the Bills were determined not to just win their second game of the season but to gain a measure of payback for their humiliating Super Bowl loss. The Cowboys, for their part, were merely trying to get untracked after losing their opening game. And just like their Super Bowl game, turnovers played a big part in this encounter. Only this time it was the Cowboys who lost two fumbles and Aikman who threw two interceptions.

It had been a discouraging day for Dallas. Late in the fourth quarter, the Cowboys drove 98 yards to tie the game only to watch a rookie punt returner, Kevin Williams, basically hand the game to Buffalo, as Tasker recovered the loose ball to set up Steve Christie's decisive 35-yard field goal.

Less than three minutes remained, and the Bills were clinging to a 13–10 lead. All their points were the result of two fumbles and an interception of Aikman in the first quarter. Despite the intense heat, Buffalo's offense never really got hot that afternoon. The Bills managed only 68 yards offensively in the second half and only 229 for the game. Buffalo was aided, in no small part, by two field goals that Lin Elliott botched, one a gimme from 30 yards. It would be the kicker's last game in a Dallas uniform. And he stood by on the sidelines as Aikman drove the Cowboys down the field in the final minutes when a field goal would have tied the game. But by then Jimmy Johnson had lost all faith in Elliott's ability to even kick an extra point.

So with time running out and faced with a second-and-4 from the Buffalo 11-yard line, Aikman tried to connect one final time with his big tight end, Jay Novacek, in the end zone. Novacek had already caught eight passes, but this time a backup safety for the Bills, Matt Darby, stepped inside Novacek and collided with the receiver just as the blistering pass reached Novacek's left shoulder. The ball popped into the air, and it was Darby who made a diving catch. It was his first NFL interception and secured the game for Buffalo.

The Cowboys, who had lost only nine fumbles in the entire previous season, had now amassed six. And to a man, the Cowboys knew Smith was the reason they were now 0–2, a hole that no team had ever overcome to go and win the Super Bowl. As scorching as it was on the field, tempers were even hotter in the Dallas dressing room. Charles Haley, the fiery defensive end, smashed a hole in a wall with his helmet and, as he walked past the locker of Emmitt's understudy, Derrick Lassic, yelled: "We'll never win with a rookie running back." Then Haley shouted, "We need to either get Emmitt here, or they've got to get rid of him." Safety Bill Bates said, "There's a huge cloud hanging over the team."

The quarterback, who was forced to throw 45 passes—more than he had in any game, was more measured in his assessment. "That's not how we've had success in the past," Aikman said. "We've had success being a balanced football team. I can say with complete certainty [that not having Smith] has been a distraction for this football team." But Jones, seemingly in denial at his team's predicament, had already been talking that day about reducing his offer to Smith, claiming that his former star running back had already missed two games, and his offer had been calculated on 16 work weeks. "I can look you straight in the eye," he told reporters in his private suite before the game, "and tell you we may have less flexibility than we've ever had because we may very well be reducing the offer. We're missing ballgames, and that has to be taken into consideration. The more games he misses, the less dollars he will ultimately get. That's a fact."

It was also a fact that with or without Smith, Dallas lost the game, and Buffalo won. And the Bills were treating this as much more than a typical early-season win. "The Cowboys know how it feels now to turn the ball over," Kelly all but crowed. "This sure feels good after all the talk that went on about last January." Pressed further, Kelly was asked how much he had thought about last year's debacle in Pasadena during this game. "Zero," he said. But to reporters, his eyes said more. "Now they know how it feels when you turn the ball over and lose like we did in the Super Bowl," Kelly went on to say. "They know they're not 35 points better."

Even Levy expressed how difficult it had been to put that loss behind him. "This one has special meaning," the coach admitted. "They beat us in the Super Bowl and did it with turnovers. We scored all of our points off turnovers."

But a 13-point output hardly equated with a 52-point blowout —a sentiment shared by many of the Bills. "This doesn't make me feel any better about last season," Tasker said. "But it makes me feel better about this year. I must admit we did come here with some emotional baggage. Well, we checked our bags." Cornelius Bennett, the great Bills linebacker, wasn't about to get too hyped up about this win. "Our defensive philosophy was totally different without Emmitt in there," he said. "We could just sit back and invite them to throw deep balls."

And no knew better than Thomas just how diminished the Cowboys were without his great rival. "Emmitt could have made the difference for Dallas," Thomas said. "In the Super Bowl, they controlled the ball. They didn't do that today."

As the game drew to a close, Jones could barely be seen in the tunnel leading to his team's dressing room—far from his familiar celebratory presence along the Dallas sideline. However, on this day the owner stood beneath a banner that read: "Emmitt Smith. There Is No Substitute."

Afterward, Johnson, fighting back emotion, said, "We're fighting a lot of things right now. We're fighting more than the game itself." Smith's holdout wasn't the coach's only problem. His place-kicker, Elliott, had struggled through the first two games of the season, missing two field goals in four attempts and an extra point. Johnson cut him the next day and brought in Eddie Murray.

But massive offensive tackle Nate Newton said the contract dispute was destroying the team. "You keep seeing on film all the big plays Emmitt made for us last year," he said. "I'm burning for last year's film. I'm tired of talking about Emmitt." Fullback Daryl Johnston lined up directly in front of Smith during most formations.

"Two weeks ago people were talking about us like we're a dynasty," Johnston said. "Now they talk like we're all done."

But the Cowboys weren't finished. Four days later, Smith signed a four-year contract worth a reported $13.6 million, which made him the highest paid running back in football history. It also made Dallas a complete team again. When Smith returned to the field against the Cardinals in Phoenix, Arizona, for his first game of the season, it was in the second half. There were 22 minutes left in the game, and he carried the ball only eight times for 45 yards, but the Cowboys won and they were on their way. On the final Sunday of the season, Dallas came to the Meadowlands to face the Giants. Each team had an 11–4 record, and the NFC East title and top seed in the conference playoffs would belong to the winner.

In the first half, Smith separated his right shoulder but continued to play on in obvious pain to everyone watching in Giants Stadium and on national TV. In what was to be the hallmark game of his Hall of Fame career, the durable and redoubtable running back ran for 168 yards, the final 41 coming on the game winning drive in overtime as Dallas prevailed 16–13. In so doing, Smith achieved his third straight league rushing title and won the admiration of football fans everywhere.

After the game, and for the only time in his broadcast career, John Madden went to a locker room—to congratulate Smith. The Hall of Fame coach, who had won a Super Bowl with the Oakland Raiders, later wrote: "It was one of the toughest efforts I've ever seen by any football player in any game." It was also the performance that would provide Smith and his teammates with a week off before the playoffs—a time to heal and get ready for another run for the championship of all football.

Ultimately, Buffalo took care of business in the regular season. They went on to take the AFC East title with a win in Philadelphia in Week 15. With a 12–4 record, the Bills captured their fourth AFC East title in five years and secured a bye week and home-field advantage throughout the playoffs.

In their bruising divisional playoff game against the Raiders, the Bills suffered some key injuries: Metzelaars dislocated a finger, and Thomas sustained a concussion. Buffalo trailed 17–6 late in the first half but came back to win on a Kelly touchdown pass in the fourth quarter.

The following week, the Bills were playing for history. A win over the Kansas City Chiefs—led by the great Joe Montana, who had already won four Super Bowls with the San Francisco 49ers— and Buffalo would become the first team to win four straight AFC crowns.

Against the Chiefs, Thomas ran for two touchdowns to spark Buffalo to a 20–6 lead late in the first half. Montana then drove the Chiefs to the Bills 5-yard line, only to be intercepted by Henry Jones in the end zone. At the outset of the third quarter, Montana was clobbered by Bruce Smith and Jeff Wright and was knocked out of the game with a concussion. The future Hall of Fame quarterback was carried off the field, after which his career belonged to the history books. Late in the game, Thomas ran for his third touchdown and the final score in a 30–13 victory. Indeed, the day belonged to Thomas, who gained 186 yards on 33 carries. More important, he had earned the right to face off in the Super Bowl with another great runner in Smith.

A Super Bowl rematch (the first ever) had the press in a frenzy, and once again the Bills would face a barrage of questions about destiny, confidence, and all their past failures. "We don't want to just go. We want to go and win it," Kelly said, echoing previous years.

What more could be said?

The defending champion Cowboys were young and an emerging dynasty. Their offense was explosive and powerful, and their defense was physical and fast. For the Bills the game would either be a triumph of will over adversity or one more excruciating defeat that would cast a stigma on them forever. And the team from the Rust Belt was beginning to show its wear and tear from years of tense games. Indeed, if you tallied up all the postseason games the Bills played these four seasons, the number you would come up with was 13, almost an additional full season.

The Cowboys were every bit as motivated and determined as the Bills were. Aikman had suffered a concussion in the NFC Championship Game, a convincing 38–21 Dallas triumph, but vowed to play in the Super Bowl. "You only get to play in so many Super Bowls," Aikman said, trying to rationalize his situation.

"I think our guys were motivated," Johnson recalled. "The concern that we had again was for that no-huddle offense. We'd only had one week to prepare between the NFC Championship Game and the Super Bowl, and so I was more concerned the second time around more than I really was the first time around."

Emotions ran high on both sides of the ball, and the stage was set for an epic battle.

Unfortunately, turnovers would continue to haunt the Bills in the big game. Not long after Christie connected on a Super Bowl–record 54-yard field goal to tie the game at three, Thomas fumbled after catching a shovel pass at midfield, helping Dallas to a 6–3 lead.

The turnover was the result of Johnson's observant eye. During Super Bowl week, television news crews and reporters are briefly allowed into practice to get some shots and interviews and make some observations before the workout is closed for teams to put in new plays. "I was actually watching *SportsCenter* that week and I see Jim Kelly and Thurman Thomas in shorts," Johnson remembered. "You know, when they allow reporters to go in the first 10, 15 minutes during the stretch to get some video. It was during that time. The cameras, the TV people were filming Jim and Thurman, the two of them in shorts, almost like playing around. But the two of them almost simulated a shovel pass.

"So I went to my defensive coordinator, Butch Davis. I said, 'Butch, have they run a shovel pass this year?' And we went and looked back on the computer printouts, and they hadn't. And I remembered that we had been hurt, our defense had been hurt by the shovel pass by the Miami Dolphins in the preseason that year. And so we started practicing versus the shovel." Johnson revels in his detective work to this day. "I told Jim Kelly that story later on. I don't think he was as amused as I was."

After the botched shovel pass, Buffalo fought back and Thomas scored from four yards out to give the Bills a 10–6 lead early in the second quarter. After Christie added another field goal, Buffalo took a 13–6 lead into the locker room. "At halftime everyone was high-fiving one another in the locker room and saying we're finally going to come away with a victory," Jim Ritcher, the offensive guard, said. "We thought, 'We're finally going to push through and get this win.' It was almost like no one wanted to see us back in the Super Bowl because we had lost three of them, but this one was going to redeem us. Finally, we were going to get the one we wanted."

Dallas may have been behind, but there was no sense of panic in their locker room. "Oh, I just didn't want the game to get away from us," Johnson remembered. "We had dominated them so much the year before, and I felt like we had the better team. So I talked to the team and said, 'We're gonna come back out and we're gonna run the football. We're gonna pump it to Emmitt and take back control of the game by taking it down the field and running the football. In the first half we hadn't established our running game like we had in the past.'"

Talley couldn't wait to get back out on the field for the second half. "We had them right where we wanted them," he remembered. "We were playing our game. We were finally comfortable. We got so emotionally charged up, and you have to sit and wait. I know halftime in the Super Bowl is 15 minutes longer, but that day it seemed like it was Chinese water torture, waiting on the game to start the third quarter. I couldn't wait to get back out there. And we did what a lot of teams and a lot of good teams do. We had a bit of an emotional letdown in the third quarter—and that right there was the turning point. It was just one or two plays."

The fatal blow was struck in the very first minute of the second half. Leon Lett stripped the ball out of Thomas' hands, and Cowboys safety James Washington picked it up and maneuvered 46 yards into the end zone. The score was 13–13. But, for all intents and purposes Dallas was really leading 13–13. That's how stunned and deflated the Bills were.

Metzelaars couldn't believe it was happening again. "It just kind of demoralized us," he said. "We never got back out of it. We never got back into the game."

The game was still tied. That's the message Levy was trying to convey to his team along the sideline. But Metzelaars believes the mood swing was insurmountable. "It really changed the momentum, really changed our mind-set," he says. "We were playing good and then, we're like, 'Oh, no' following the turnover. And you think of the Super Bowl the year before. Doubt? There's no question those things play in your mind. Certainly with the heightened circumstances of playing in the Super Bowl, playing in our fourth Super Bowl, and we haven't won one yet, all that stuff rolling around in your mind, playing with you, the pressure of it. The media and everybody saying to you, 'Gosh, this is your fourth time. When are you ever going to win?' Some telling us, 'Hey, if you're not going to win the Super Bowl, don't even go to the playoffs.' You hear it over and over. I think it did weigh on the team a little bit."

After that, the Bills offense sputtered, and the Cowboys offense promptly took complete control of the game. It was just the way Johnson had drawn it up at halftime. With Smith leading the way, the Cowboys methodically drove 64 yards in eight plays to go in front 20–13. They never looked back.

It had been a monumental year for Smith. He began the season as a holdout and then suffered a separated shoulder in the final week as he carried his team past the Giants in overtime at the Meadowlands for the NFC East title. Now he was carrying them again, rushing seven times in their opening drive of the second half, gaining 61 yards, culminating with a 15-yard run into the end zone.

Along the Buffalo sideline, Ritcher could only watch Emmitt in awe and stunned silence. "It seemed like Emmitt Smith sort of took it upon himself that he was going to win that ballgame," Ritcher said. "I saw our guys still getting through their linemen at the line of scrimmage, but he was still getting the ball and plowing through there. You know, three, four yards. Three, four guys on his back and he was just doing it. And I'm on the sideline just watching it and it was amazing. Such determination. It was: no matter what, he was just going to carry that ball and win the ballgame."

Early in the fourth quarter with Dallas still ahead 20–13, Washington intercepted Kelly at the Bills 46 and returned it to the 34. Smith quickly pounced, and his second touchdown put the Cowboys up by two touchdowns with 10 minutes remaining. It was all over but the shouting. Dallas would go on to win back-to-back titles and become the first Super Bowl champion to have opened the season with two losses.

The Cowboys also had the pleasure of contemplating which Super Bowl was more rewarding. "The first one was very rewarding because it was my first Super Bowl," Johnson said recently. "The second one was rewarding in that there's not a lot of teams repeating because of all the problems you have bringing back a Super Bowl champion. And plus we had problems with Emmitt having a two-game holdout. We weren't the same team [without him]. I really hadn't prepared our offense to go out there and play without him. And so I put that on myself, not being totally prepared."

Not since the loss to the Giants had the Bills felt so much despair. They had come so far, come so close with the finish line in sight. Only 30 minutes separated them from immortality. Now they feared their legacy would be forever tainted. "We thought we were the better team," Ritcher said, "but you have to prove it for 60 minutes, not just for 30 minutes." The high-fives? "Yeah, that was probably part of the problem. We actually thought we had won it before we had. Not that we didn't go out with the same intensity, but determination..." He has never gotten the image of Emmitt's fighting for every yard out of his mind.

Smith ran for 92 yards in the second half, 132 for the game on 30 carries. He had led the league in rushing and was named the season and Super Bowl MVP. Perhaps most important, he did not fumble in the big game. On the other side, it was the same old story for Buffalo. Three turnovers resulted in 17 points, once more equaling the margin of defeat.

The loss was especially disheartening for Emmitt's counterpart, Thomas. "There is no doubt the key play to the game was my fumble," he acknowledged afterward. "James Washington took the ball the other way, and that was the game."

Beebe still remembers how the life seemed to go out of his team, following Thomas's big fumble, how all the confidence they felt coming out of the locker room at halftime vanished as soon as Washington crossed the goal line. "We go into that locker room at halftime feeling pretty good," Beebe said. "We're handling the line of scrimmage of the Dallas Cowboys at that time. I felt comfortable we can do this, we can do that. The coaches felt very comfortable, and the players were positive and everything was good. And we had the ball first in the second half and we said, 'Let's go out there and get them. Let's get more than a one touchdown lead and let's put this game away. It's our game.' And so what do we do?

"Well, within a few plays Thurman fumbles it by Leon Lett knocking the ball out of his hands, and James Washington picks it up and scores the touchdown. Well, you come to the sideline and I promise you, you thought we were down 30. I mean guys were throwing helmets, guys were just complaining, here we effin' go again. They were cussing, swearing, and nobody was positive. Nobody was positive. Not one coach, not one player. It's tied, and you would have thought we're down 30. What happened the rest of the game? We don't score another point."

The final series of crushing blows were delivered by Smith, a true champion, and they came in sustained flurries, like an uncontested barrage of body blows in a heavyweight title fight designed to sap a challenger of his strength and drain his spirit.

"Playing defense and tackling somebody, I promise you it's all attitude, it's all emotion," Beebe said. "You got to want to go knock his head off. You have to play that way. And offensively it's a little bit different, but you still have to play with great emotion and passion. You have to be able to concentrate on the snap count, catching the football, throwing the ball, running the football, hanging on to the ball, not fumbling. And our attitude went right in the tank. Same team, different attitude."

As they trudged out of the Georgia Dome, the Bills began to face the stark reality. Future shock, even. They had reached the last stop on their road to the Super Bowl. And once more they had choked in the big game. "I just remember walking off the field thinking, 'Goddamn son of a bitch! I just had another bite of this apple and I still haven't swallowed it,'" remembered Talley, who never missed a game in his 12 seasons with the Bills. "That's all I could think about. Goddamn, I had four bites of that apple and I still haven't swallowed it. I still think about it to this day."

"You start to wonder," Beebe said, "after three and four, 'Gosh are we ever going to get here again? Are we ever going to have these opportunities?' When you go through it you think to yourself, 'On the one hand we're going to do this again. And on the other hand, Jesus, man, are we ever going to get back?' You think about how hard it is to get there. Only two teams go."

"It's a bitter loss," Levy conceded in the aftermath. "I sort of don't want to be consoled by people who are well-wishers."

Kelly struggled to rationalize what had happened. "We work so hard to make it this far in the season to where we are today and you always think, 'Why did we deserve to lose and play the way we played today?'"

Unlike the two previous Super Bowls in which he had been knocked out, Kelly made it through this game. But being able to contribute a full 60 minutes didn't make the loss any less agonizing. Kelly certainly knew he wasn't getting any younger, and the youthful Cowboys weren't going anywhere soon.

The Bills had wanted to win it as much as they had wanted anything in their lives. Not just for themselves and each other, but for all their fans who had been through so much with them over the years.

"I think what happened is after they lost the first one—it was such a heartbreaker—the pressure was just unbelievable," said Bob Kochinski, the Buffalo TV reporter. "You know getting there was always the challenge, and once they got there they just weren't the same team they were during the season. They played a good game against the Giants and a good half against the Cowboys [in] the last game, and then the wheels started to fall off. When Thurman Thomas fumbled that ball and it was returned for a touchdown, even though it was a tie game, I think all of us from Buffalo felt like, 'Here we go. They're gonna lose.' And I talked to players on that team, and they thought, they sat there, the monkey on their back weighed about 10,000 pounds, and they just couldn't overcome that kind of mental handicap being there that many times and coming up short."

A feeling of disbelief almost came over their fans in the Georgia Dome that night. Donn Bartz remembers the feeling. "We just felt we're due," he said. "And there we are, and we're winning this game. We're feeling we've got it. It's building up inside, 'Hey, we're going to be champions and it turns around in the second half.' Thurman gets stripped. It just knocks the wind right out of your sails. Did they choke? I don't know. How do you define that? It just wasn't in the cards. It wasn't in the cards that we went four times and lost four times. But you keep cheering for them."

"The Super Bowl in Atlanta," Peter Nussbaum remembered from his days fresh out of college, "that was the first time you felt like there was just a curse. It was never meant to be. I remember defending it that I'll take four Super Bowl losses over one Super Bowl appearance and a win any day of the week. All the winning, week in and week out and throughout the playoffs, only to lose the ultimate game. It was still great."

Ange Coniglio, the engineer who lives in the small town of Amherst, one block from the city line, says, "If anybody asks me where I'm from, I say Buffalo. I'm a Buffalo kid." Ange finally made it to a Super Bowl, that game down in Georgia. "I didn't know what a thrill it was until I looked up and saw all the flags of all the teams that had been in the Super Bowl, one for every year. And to see the Bills flag up there four years in a row," he said. "I don't think anybody will ever do that again. It was a terrific accomplishment, and that's why I think they were one of the best teams in professional football history."

He remembers watching a game on TV years after the Bills had played in their last Super Bowl. Aikman was calling the game on FOX, and he gave those vanquished Bills a shout-out: "You've got to give that team credit. They got there four times in a row. You can't believe how difficult it is to get there even one year. And they got there four years in a row."

It made Coniglio swell with pride. It had to make everyone in Buffalo who was listening proud to hear that salute from one of the game's greatest champions. "I think Buffalo fans are proud of them for that," Coniglio said. "That was quite a team. It was a pleasure to watch. It was a great experience all around and it touched all of Buffalo, all of western New York, all of southern Ontario. Everybody was a Bills fan. The old cliché—it's a northeast town, a Rust Belt town, a blue-collar town. And that's the kind of team that it was. They personified that. And the fact that they could go back four years and give it their all, only a player could tell you how disappointing it was not to have won one of those things."

The disappointment lingers for all of them, but the memories never fade. Perspective is what Mark Kelso takes away from it. "The great lesson in perseverance, and I think one of the things that was great about Marv, was that you hope football wasn't the most important thing in your life," he said. "It was important because it was your job, and we brought enjoyment to a lot of people that it was important to—hundreds of thousands of people here in Buffalo. And it was that contact that enabled you to play so well on gameday."

Kelly would give anything to have won one. For his team. For their fans. For Buffalo. "I don't look at it where we let the city down," Kelly says today as he looks back on his career. "I look at it, yeah, I let myself down. I wanted to win it just as bad. But I wanted to win more for them than I did for myself. But as long as you go out there and you do what you're supposed to do and you give it 100 percent and you fight to the end, I do not hang my head low. Win or lose, I always walk with my head held up high, my shoulders back, and proud to say, 'I'm a Buffalo Bill.'"

CHAPTER 12 | Don Beebe's Salvation

THREE YEARS LATER after joining the Green Bay Packers as a free agent, Don Beebe believes he discovered what had been missing during the Buffalo Bills Super Bowl years. The Packers, with Brett Favre at quarterback, jumped out to a quick 10–0 lead against the New England Patriots in Super Bowl XXXI. Green Bay was a heavy favorite—by two touchdowns—and it looked like this Super Bowl was going to be yet another blowout for the NFC.

"We're thinking we're feeling pretty good," Beebe said. "Next thing you know, Drew Bledsoe goes *boom, boom,* two long plays. They got two touchdowns real quick. It's not even the second quarter, and we're down 14–10. I can tell you right now, Buffalo goes to that sideline, [thinking] we're done. We'd have thought, 'Oh, no, here we go again.' But Green Bay's sideline? Way positive. I think about the leaders on that football team: Reggie White, Eugene Robinson, LeRoy Butler, myself at that time, and I'm thinking, 'There's no way I'm losing another one.' And everybody was positive. I remember comments like, 'Guys were all right. Let's just keep doing what we're doing. Got a long game left. Just keep making the plays.' Next thing you know, the halftime score was 27–14 Green Bay. We just put the game away."

The Packers were so confident, so secure in their ability that even now Beebe hardly remembers that the Patriots had rallied and trailed by only a touchdown before Desmond Howard took a kick-off 99 yards late in the third quarter to truly put the game away. "Attitude and emotion, that was the difference between the two teams," Beebe said of those men he played with in Buffalo and Green Bay. "We just could not handle the emotion of the game itself in Buffalo. We could handle all the other games with the emotions. I mean, good God, we're down 35–3, we handled that emotion just fine. But when it came to the Super Bowl, for some reason we struggled winning the game because of our emotions. We got too down on ourselves when we made a mistake."

Maybe it all went back to that first Super Bowl in Tampa. Kelly and Thomas and the Bills driving down the field and Norwood lining up for the field goal that would change the fortune of a franchise and the outlook of a city. "If we had won that first one," Beebe said, "I think it would have built so much confidence in us that we would have rolled to four in a row. I really believe that. Because talentwise I really believe that we were far superior than a lot of teams we played. And I'm not trying to take away from the teams that we played. They were great teams. Every team in the NFL's got great talent, but we just had something of that chemistry about that team; we just loved each other. And the organization and the fan base was second to none. And I think that would have carried us over."

But that fateful kick drifted wide right, and things never seemed to go right for the Bills in another Super Bowl thereafter. The Bills had come as close as you could to winning a Super Bowl, so they knew they could do it. And that first loss also instilled a confidence and determination that enabled them to get back to three ensuing championship games. All you had to do was look at their gritty wins against John Elway and Joe Montana and the Houston Oilers. Then they ran up against the Washington Redskins and Dallas Cowboys and something happened.

"We had the resiliency in that we were able to block out what had happened to us the previous year and focus on what was in front of us and to be able to come together as a team and accomplish things that were seen as almost impossible to do," Kelly said. "When you go to four in a row, you always think you have a chance. We got excited like most teams would get excited going back. Pressure? There's always pressure on the quarterback to succeed. That goes with the job. There are things that happened during the course of a game. Super Bowl XXVI against Washington, I open the third quarter up and I throw an interception—and those things can hurt you. The missed field goal in the first one. And the Dallas game where we had the fumble returned for the touchdown. That's three turning points in games that decide what the outcome's gonna be."

Right before the kickoff in the Bills' last Super Bowl in the Georgia Dome, Beebe gathered his teammates together. "I was like, 'We are not losing this game,' and this is out of character for me," he says. "I brought them together and was getting into them. I got everybody up. *We are not losing this football game.* I was so focused. I was so ready, the ball was like a watermelon for cryin' out loud! I could have caught any ball thrown my way that day. That's how I felt. So when you have that kind of spirit about you and then you still lose, and the way you lost getting killed again—it's devastating. I must say that was the most dejecting loss of my life at any time, at any level."

If you love the game so much that it can break your heart, then you never get over it. It stays with you a lifetime, and nothing can change that. Not even winning a Super Bowl.

Don Beebe realized his dream of winning the big game in the Superdome of New Orleans on a Sunday night in January 1997. The Green Bay Packers had just won the Super Bowl, and Favre doled out high praise for a wide receiver who did not catch a single pass that evening: "We would not have won Super Bowl XXXI without Don Beebe." It was a testament to Beebe's attitude and emotion as much as it was his talent and ability.

During that celebration Beebe was ushered onto a podium and accorded the opportunity to hold the Vince Lombardi Trophy. "How do you feel after losing four and finally winning one?" the press clamored. Beebe remembered, "I kind of got emotional and broke down. I said, 'I'll be honest with you, all I can think about right now is Marv Levy, Jim Kelly, Bill Polian, John Butler. All the fans in western New York. Ralph Wilson, all my old teammates out there. What I really wish is that every one of them could have been experiencing this with me right now because they all deserve this.'"

CHAPTER 13 | The End of the Run

THE BILLS DID not make it back to the Super Bowl in the 1994 season. They did not even make it back to the playoffs. A proud team, they were defiant to the end, believing they would win their last couple of games of the regular season to get into the postseason and then, well, you know the rest. They would somehow claw their way back to the big dance and get one more shot at the glass slipper.

"It hit us after Week 15 when we had to win our last two to get into the playoffs and then we didn't do it," Pete Metzelaars remembers. "That was a shock because when we needed to win games before, we'd win games—other than the Super Bowl. Not getting it done in that situation was disappointing, shocking."

In early December it still looked like they might stage another late-season rally and have a chance to reach a fifth straight Super Bowl. Playing in Miami, the Bills suddenly looked like the Bills of old as they erupted for five touchdowns in the first 20 minutes of the second half. Jim Kelly and Don Beebe and Andre Reed were connecting for home runs all over Joe Robbie Stadium. The 42–31 victory raised their record to 7–6 and lifted their spirits as they made their way back home.

But the following week in Buffalo—the third to last game of the regular season—the Bills and Kelly took a severe hit and simply looked old and beaten up as if they had finally taken their final blow. Trailing Minnesota 21–17 and with only a minute and a half left in the game and desperate to make a play, Kelly was hit and fell to the ground. The ligaments in his left knee were sprained yet again, and he had to be taken off the field on a cart. Later he left the locker room in a wheel chair. "I heard him moaning," center Kent Hull said. "You learn that moan after 12 years. You know somebody is hurt."

The very next Sunday in Buffalo, the Bills' Super Bowl run would end, uncermoniously. Although Frank Reich guided the Bills to an early 17–3 lead, the day quickly became dismal as rain turned to snow, and Drew Bledsoe and the New England Patriots scored the next 38 points. Final score: New England 41, Buffalo 17. All over. The loss eliminated the Bills from any possibility of making the playoffs for the first time in seven years.

For Marv Levy it was nearly as devastating an end to the season as he had endured in the previous four years. "From my standpoint, other than the Super Bowl lossses, I can't remember a game where I've been more disappointed or feel worse about than this one," he told the assembled reporters. "It's a feeling of sadness that we are not the team we have been. Reality tells you that. But I am not going to take that sense of sadness to the rocking chair on the porch and say, 'Boy, those were the good old days.' I don't want to give in to that and I won't."

Once more he had lost to Bill Parcells who was now in the process of building the Patriots into a Super Bowl team. But Parcells, who coached the New York Giants to two Super Bowl titles, could often be blunt and standoffish, seemed touched by the occasion and was unusually gracious in his postgame remarks. "To come here and beat these guys in this place, to put them away, that's something not too many teams have done in the past few years," he said. "I know the season is over for them. But it doesn't end without a tremendous respect for what these guys here accomplished."

The Bills simply ran out of gas. They pressed down on the accelerator, but nothing was left in the tank. Their season would end with one more loss, a meaningless 10–9 defeat at the Indianapolis Colts, to finish 7–9. "It was a little bit strange," Metzelaars said. "We just never could get anything going. You didn't feel that way when you're in the middle of it, but you're mentally and physically worn out. We didn't make the playoffs, had a chance to win our last two games of the year to still get in and we just couldn't get it done."

It was a hard fall for Buffalo. Battered and bruised and sidelined at the end of what seemed like their longest season, Kelly found it hard to accept the Bills were not going back for a fifth Super Bowl. "You never know," Kelly said. "That's what you play them for: to be there at the end. I always feel it's our moment. You don't know my passion, how I feel, but I always thought it was our moment. As long as I was quarterback, I thought we had a chance to go back. You gotta have great players around you, but I always thought we had a great chance to go back."

He wasn't that far off. The Bills had become a Super Bowl team that summer day in 1986 when he arrived in Buffalo, breathing excitement into a team and a city that had been downtrodden for far too long. It wasn't long before he won the respect of his teammates and the hearts of western New York with his grit and his talent and his will to win. You could knock him down, but he'd get right back up. He'd yell and swear and inspire everyone who saw him play. As much as anyone who ever wore a Bills uniform, Jim Kelly was a true Buffalonian. "The ultimate blue collar quarterback," Bill Polian called him.

"If they were to make a movie about the life of John Wayne, Jim Kelly ought to play the part," Marv Levy said.

"More than anything it was a work ethic," Kelly said. "Anybody who came to Buffalo knew Marv Levy was a big-time key. Having a guy like Bill Polian, a guy that was blue-collar, we knew he wanted the working man to come in here and be a part of this. And Marv was always saying he wants 'character' people. Self-motivated players, that's what he looked for. That's what he believed in. We had resiliency in our hearts. The will to win? We had it, and Marv was responsible for it. Even though we didn't win the Super Bowl, the work ethic we instilled in each and every practice, and the work ethic that Marv Levy instilled in each and every one of his players is one of the key ingredients for our success."

There was a game against the Steelers in the early years before the Bills were a playoff team when Kelly took "a tremendous shot late in the first half," according to Polian, "I swore he broke his wrist. I said, 'Oh God, here goes the season.' And Frank Reich, of course, wasn't Frank Reich at that time. So off Jim goes, and they take him into the locker room, and the stadium is deathly silent. Deathly silent, just as quiet as it could be. And play resumes, and we're going along, maybe there's a couple of minutes left in the half, and down the tunnel he comes and he's got a wrap around his wrist and he jogs back out. And the place just erupted. And he put his hat on and out he went back to work."

And the Bills never took a Sunday off. They did something no other team has ever done in the history of the National Football

League. They went to four straight Super Bowls. Who knows when or if it will ever be done again?

Wherever those Buffalo Bills players go, all around America, fans always come up to them and salute them on what they accomplished. The conversation usually goes the same way: "I'm one of those fans who didn't want you to go back to another Super Bowl. Oh, no, not the Buffalo Bills again." Or "I'm one of those reporters who wrote, 'Anyone but Buffalo.'" And then they will pay tribute to them. What the old players usually hear, Kelly said, goes something like this: "What you guys accomplished is amazing. That you guys were able to go back four years in a row and not win is something. It's something if you had something to build on, like a win here and there, but to be there and pull together as a team, the resilience you guys had to do that, and reach that goal, even though you didn't win, is amazing."

As Marv Levy says, "There's only one way you can never lose a Super Bowl game: don't go." After all these years, the coach is still asked if there's a stigma on his team. "Oh, I don't know. I don't know." Then a trace of bitterness creeps into his voice. "I'll leave that up to others. Look, we would have like to have won them all. Or one or two or three. We didn't. We just didn't play well enough to come out on top. I'll remember the good. I'll remember the great people I was with. I'll remember the resilience of getting to the game. I'll remember the never-say-quit attitude. I'll remember there was never shred of blame placed on anybody else. I'll remember the support of our fans. I'll remember the excitement of not knowing what the outcome is going to be. Sure, we would have preferred to win 'em, but we can't change it now. So it's time to remember all the good things that got us there."

Marv Levy spent 47 years coaching football players, his last 12 in Buffalo, which he calls the most gratifying time of his career. On a football field he loved to ask his players: "Where would you rather be than right here, right now?" If he didn't live for the game, then he sure did love it. In the words of Polian, "He took a mediocre team and made it great."

And when the coach thinks back on all those gamedays, not a single one stands out. There was no pinnacle in his career. The world only spins forward. "I have to admit it wasn't one moment. It was a journey," Levy said. "Just the ability to fight your way back, and I don't know if it really clicks in your consciousness, but 32 highly talented teams go to training camp, hungering to get to the playoffs. Twelve of them finally make it, and 11 of them have their season end with a loss. There was a period when we mourned. We didn't just shrug it off. It hurt for awhile. But they didn't continue to just lie there in the fetal position and just whimper. The way they'd go back to work and be supportive of each other, it was unique."

One of the game's great winners, Parcells, considers Levy and his Bills teams among the most admirable in football history. "They had a great run those Buffalo Bills," he said. "Some of the great names in NFL history played there. I just have an awful lot of respect for their players and Coach Levy and what Coach Levy and his staff did. It's pretty remarkable. And what they accomplished in the league and getting to four straight Super Bowls. That was really pretty amazing. We sure as hell couldn't do it. Oh my God, that's impossible to do, but he did it."

"I can't speak for them because I don't know what the ramifications are, were, because I wasn't privilege to those," Parcells says looking back on the aftermath of that epic 20–19 championship game. "I know it was a devastating defeat for them just like it was a very exhilarating victory for us. After that conference championship game they played against the Raiders, that was so impressive and then coming in there against us and not being able to finish. I'm certainly not speaking for them, but I'm certain it's a little depressing."

Twenty-two Buffalo Bills were members of all four teams that went to the Super Bowl. Mark Kelso has the rings commemorating each one of those games in safekeeping. "I have a box of Super Bowl rings that has five spots," he says. "And I've got four rings. And when people ask 'What's the fifth one for? And I say, 'It's the one we didn't win.' The one we still thought we should have had.' And we always felt it was gonna be our time. Would I trade one ring for four? Can't tell you that. I can tell you I'd trade two for four."

In the end the fourth loss may have been the toughest to accept because it marked the end of the run.

"Oh, I think they had an excellent organization and an excellent team," Jimmy Johnson said recently. "I think it was a good run, but again if you don't win the Super Bowl, it's not a great run. It's all about the rings."

One November after his retirement from the NFL, Kelly decided he wanted to go see a big football game and experience it like a real fan. He had been in big games all his life, from the inside looking out. Now he wanted to see it from the other side—buy a ticket, tailgate in the parking lot, have a few beers and hot dogs, yell yourself hoarse for your team. So he asked Dennis DiPaolo, if he could make it happen. The game Kelly wanted to see was Ohio State–Michigan, only the biggest rivalry in college football at the time. "I said, 'That's impossible,'" DiPaolo remembered. "That's like trying to get a ticket to the Super Bowl." Kelly was insistent that he try. Kelly didn't want to hear that. "They told me you can," he said. "See if you can get tickets or something."

"I go, *Madonne*," DiPaolo said, invoking the Blessed Mother.

Maybe it was an act from God, or one of his disciples, but DiPaolo was able to get a pair of tickets, and off they went. It was one of the greatest times they had together. "He had never experienced a big time game like that," DiPaolo said. "He played in Super Bowls and all that stuff, but to be a fan—he wanted to experience it. So we go to the game, and there's like more than 100,000 fans outside. He goes, 'This is what it's like?' And I go, 'Jim, this is what those Super Bowls were like when you were in that locker room. It was so exciting. Bands are playing. People are cheering. People are going wild.' And then he says he wants to get into the stadium early and walking around he goes, 'You could almost feel it, Oh my God.' I said, 'Jim, all those years you're focused as a player. Us fans, we wish we could be you. But we enjoyed every moment of it, just watching you guys perform.'"

For the people of Buffalo, the Bills, and their fans, the memories last forever. It's a cold morning as they get out of their cars in the parking lots, smoke billows from tailpipes everywhere. The smell of barbecue and beer fills the air. Fans put on their layers of down clothing. Everywhere you look, everyone is smiling and happy and getting their game face on.

Maybe their Bills never had that one shining moment that defines all other champions, but *man,* did they come close.

There were two minutes and six seconds left when the Bills began that final drive against the Giants. Jim Ritcher, the offensive guard, was certain he was about to become a champion as he came off the field at the end of that drive, giving way to the offense. "We're gonna win the game,'" Ritcher remembered thinking. "This is it. We got down in field-goal range. I wasn't on the field-goal team and I came over to the sideline and I kneeled down and took off my helmet. And, of course, my face was all sweated up from the game, and I remember as they're lined up and he's just about to start his kick for the uprights, all of a sudden there wasn't a gust or anything, but I can just feel the wind increase on my face, the most sensitive part of me. And I'm just hoping as he starts his kick that he had taken into consideration that this wind had started."

That moment still gives them chills. The ball is in the air. Anything is possible.

"There was a movie, *A Family Thing*. Robert Duvall was in it and he had a line that always stuck with me," Bob Koshinski said. "Happiness is nothing more than having something to look forward to."

That's Buffalo. That's what it means to be a Buffalonian.

When Bill Polian came to Buffalo, Jerry Glanville, who coached the Houston Oilers and the Atlanta Falcons, advised him: "If you stay there more than one year, you'll be a Buffalo Bill for life." Polian says today, years after moving on to other jobs that further enhanced his résumé and reputation. "He could not have been more right." When Polian became the president of the Indianapolis Colts, he promptly selected Peyton Manning with the first overall pick in the 1998 draft. Manning is perhaps the greatest quarterback the game has produced, and when he led the Colts to a 29–17 Super Bowl victory over the Chicago Bears on February 4, 2007, in Miami, Polian was finally able to savor the moment and raise the Lombardi Trophy.

It would be the only Super Bowl Peyton would win with the Colts, and when he returned to Indianapolis with the Denver Broncos early in the 2013 season, Jim Irsay, the Colts' owner, bemoaned the fact that Peyton had delivered them only one ring.

Some people you can never satsify, but Polian is not one of them. "Our record is what it is," Polian told *USA TODAY* on the eve Peyton's return to Indianapolis. "We didn't win multiple Super Bowls. But I think we did a hell of a lot to make the city and state of Indiana proud—on and off the field. And here's the most important thing of all—and it goes unfortunately unspoken because of the focus on the Super Bowl and the failure to win more than one Super Bowl: we did it—and Peyton did it—the right way, honestly, fairly, and squarely."

And while the Bills never quite took home the gold, the same thing could be said about them, too. They got to the big dance four years in a row on chemistry, determination, and grit.

• • •

The Bills era was one for all time, a singular team that might have been even bigger winners had it not been for one one-point loss in one Super Bowl. And each and every man associated with that team remembers those golden years with great fondness. Perhaps that's why so many of them have continued to make Buffalo their home long after their playing days ended: Kelly, Steve Tasker, Kelso, Thurman Thomas, Adam Lingner, and Pete Metzelaars all remain in western New York.

Several have pursued careers in coaching, including Don Beebe, Reich, Kenneth Davis, and Metzelaars. Kelso is a high school teacher and coach and can be heard on Bills radio broadcasts. A handful of others call NFL games for the networks.

Jeff Wright works on a cattle ranch in Arizona. Howard Ballard has a farm. Cornelius Bennett represents former players. Thomas has a company that helps young athletes in Buffalo.

Ritcher is a pilot for American Airlines. Andre Reed has a foundation that raises money for kids. Kelly runs a charitable foundation in honor of his late son, Hunter, who succumbed to a rare disease as a young child.

Bruce Smith has a real estate company and also helps Operation Smile, an organization which mends cleft palates and other facial deformities in underpriviliged parts of the world. In Africa he once carried a youngster into surgery who was wearing a small Bills jersey, bearing the No. 78, Smith's old number. Imagine.

Kent Hull was the first to leave this earth. Named to three Pro Bowl teams as a center, he died of intestinal bleeding in October 2011. He was just 50 years old. "That was the first time that one of their compadres was gone," Polian said. "Far too young obviously. But it was interesting to see all the players and all the wives that came to support his wife Kay and her family. Twenty-five years later, they're still close. They'll be close forever."

At the 20th reunion of their first Super Bowl, in January 2011, Smith explained to Jerry Sullivan of *The Buffalo News* what he took from all those Super Bowls. "I don't think we realized how much that experience would impact the rest of our lives," Smith said. "It makes you a better person. It opens your eyes and makes you realize there are more important things in life than whether you win or lose. Marv tried to get us to understand that life is bigger than football. We still had a lot to learn. We've all made mistakes. We're human beings. We're flawed. For those we offended, we wish we had a chance to do it all over again. We ask for forgiveness, to make amends and move on."

And when the time came for the architect of the Super Bowl Bills to move on, Polian left as a Buffalonian and in his heart remains one even now decades later. On the day he left the Bills, following their third Super Bowl, Polian had this to say of the team he had built: "They're a very special group of men. Cherish them. You will not see their like again."

CHAPTER 14 | Hall of Fame Redemption

O F ALL THE great teams the Buffalo Bills went up against in the Super Bowl, not one squad has had more players inducted in the Pro Football Hall of Fame.

Coach Bill Parcells and his great outside linebacker Lawrence Taylor were the only members of the Giants 1990 championship team to reach the shrine in Canton, Ohio. Hall of Fame coach Joe Gibbs won his third Super Bowl title with his hallmark team in 1991. He entered, as did three of his greatest players: Darrell Green, the cornerstone of Washington's defense; Russ Grimm, the great offensive guard who played his final game that day in Minneapolis; and the durable and ever-dependable wide receiver Art Monk. The big three of the Dallas Cowboys—Troy Aikman, Emmitt Smith, and Michael Irvin—won three championships in four years, assuring the glamorous trio their place in the Hall.

By this measure time has proven Bill Polian correct in his assessment that we would not soon see men of such talent joining forces. Only those Cowboys teams of the 1990s have come close to playing on four straight super Sundays. Marv Levy, whose 12-year coaching tenure in Buffalo concluded after the 1997 season, was the first member of those great Super Bowl teams to be inducted, in 2001. The next year Jim Kelly's bronze bust was unveiled, and then in 2003 James Lofton was elected to Canton. A game-changing wide receiver, Lofton played his first nine seasons with the Green Bay Packers, followed by two years with the Los Angeles Raiders before coming to Buffalo in 1989. He took part in the Bills' first three Super Bowls.

Thurman Thomas was honored in 2007, his second year of eligibility—which was, in a twisted way, somewhat symbolic. Throughout his career the durable running back had fought for grudging respect just as he had fought to grind out every yard. And in 2009 Bruce Smith, like Kelly, was voted into the Hall in his first year of eligibility. Smith had endured 19 NFL seasons, remarkable longevity for a man who often battled against two or three opponents on every down. After 15 years in Buffalo, his career came to an end following four campaigns in Washington. But as Polian learned when he first came to Buffalo, once you spend a year there, you're a Buffalonian for life. And now, as fate would have it, the defensive end who had registered a career record 200 sacks was going into the Hall of Fame along with Buffalo's most famous citizen: the 90-year-old owner of the Bills, Ralph Wilson.

On a typically sweltering August afternoon in Canton with new members clad in canary yellow blazers for the occasion, Smith smiled and said, "As vividly as yesterday, I can remember arriving in Buffalo with Andre Reed for my first minicamp in 1985. At the first practice in the middle of May, we noticed dark clouds off at a distance. And within minutes it began to rain, hail, and snow. After 30 minutes of downpour, the sun began to shine, and I thought, 'What in the hell have I gotten myself into?'"

Finally, on the first night of February 2014, at the first cold-weather Super Bowl, which was held a few miles from New York City, Reed was voted into the Hall of Fame, the fifth player from the Super Bowl Bills to be so honored. He, too, had been a revered player in Buffalo through 15 outstanding seasons and been on all four Super Bowl teams. And like the others before him, he was overwhelmed by the reaction his election had produced. "I've had some text messages, but I never had 600 in an hour and a half," he said soon after that Super Bowl weekend when he was admitted to football's most exclusive fraternity. "That was pretty special. When I first came up, there was no Internet, no way of getting your name out there than through the team and your performance on the field. Football was my job. That was my main focus. The accolades would come if you did it on the field."

He came to Buffalo in 1985 in the same draft as Smith and Frank Reich. A fourth-round selection out of Kutztown State, Reed played college ball far from America's showcase Saturdays. But the wide receiver, who grew up in Allentown, Pennsylvania, quickly felt at home in Buffalo, a city hardly illuminated by the bright lights of bigger NFL cities. "Buffalo is so blue collar, and I'm from a blue-collar town, Allentown." Reed says. "I think both cities are similar in a way. Hard working people, man. They work hard, nine-to-five every day. They go home, they pay their bills, and take care of the family. And they love their team, they support their team, and they're there through thick and thin. That city really identified with that team. The fans really identify with those Super Bowl years even now. It's really what makes them happy. Will they ever get back to that again? Probably not. Will they ever have the same players like that again? Probably not. It only happens once in a lifetime."

Reed remembers how a veteran Buffalo receiver, Jerry Butler, took him under his wing when he first arrived in camp. "I was like a little duckling with him and I followed him everywhere and I had to do that because he was in the league five or six years. So I really became a student of the game early, watching film and studying players to get to the next level. I learned how to dissect opponents and learned how to know what's going on out there when I was out there. I was a raw kid from a small school who could run, who could catch, who was very unpolished at the time and I had to do all that studying to get better. And Jerry Butler was one of the guys I really watched to get better."

In time he became one of the most feared receivers in the league and, accordingly, was covered by the top defensive backs in the game. "I always drew the best player," he proudly recalled. "They never put their second or third guy on me. They gave me their best player. They weren't going to take their chances with somebody else. And that's the one thing you want when you step out on the field. You want respect from your opponent. And you want your opponent to know it's going to be a battle all day. I wasn't one of those players like today, 'me, me' players. Yeah I wanted the ball, but that wasn't really my main focus. My main focus was winning the football game. And if I'm involved in it, we had a better chance."

Perhaps his brightest moment occurred in what is known as the "Comeback Game." The titanic affair against the Houston Oilers when the Bills came from 32 points down as Reed caught three touchdown passes in the second half. "That game sticks out more than any other game," he still says, "because it really epitomizes what the passion for the game, what resiliency means. Of course, I had better individual games [than his eight catches for

136 yards in that playoff game], but it was a team win and all about not quitting."

Like all the great players, Reed understood you needed other great players around you to truly excel. "We had our core guys, but we had so many different guys behind us that could play for any team and start for any team and be an impact player on any team," Reed said. "If I had played for a mediocre team, I may not have had that drive. Maybe I would not have the certain kind of push that got you going every year. You never know. I just had guys that relied on me and that I relied on and I was not going to let those guys down. That's what really drove us and what we were really about."

When Reed's great running mate, Lofton, was enshrined on August 3, 2003, he spoke of the punishing conditions the Bills often played in as he sought out Kelly in the audience. "Nobody threw the ball better in the elements than Jim Kelly," Lofton said. "I'm a little disappointed it's not snowing. I was going to ask him to toss me one. Thanks, Jim."

The great wide receiver also acknowledged the impact the quarterback and Coach Levy had on his career. Lofton had joined the Bills during the regular season in 1989, and one of the rituals he was looking forward to was the coach's annual "return to the season" speech. He had heard similar pronouncements from other coaches in previous years so he expected something motivating. But Levy's address was special.

"Marv outlined what it would take for us to get home-field advantage [throughout the playoffs]," Lofton said. "And, as an older player, I sat in the front row—my vision and hearing were fading a little bit. And he said, 'What we need to do is we need to win all our conference games.' That was eight games. He said,

211

'We have eight more games, and we probably need to win five of those.' So, to me, that's 13–3. You know, I was an engineering major, so I was pretty quick with the numbers. But, I expected—the younger players sit in the back—and I expected to hear some snickering. So I peered over my left shoulder and I turned around, and everyone was just in this steely-eyed gaze. Marv Levy outlined the plan, what we needed to do. And every week he outlined how we needed to go about winning. Thank you, Marv."

Lofton believed "the game was a little simpler in the late '70s and early '80s. The defense would line up, they would come after you with a blitz, the quarterback would audible. They'd blitz eight guys. We'd have seven guys to block, so that means one guy's going to knock the snot out of the quarterback."

Then he talked about all the baggage a quarterback must carry and how much admiration he held for Kelly. "When a quarterback first comes into the league, he's normally labeled 'cocky.' As he gets a little older, he's labeled 'confident.' I can think of another 'C word', and it's 'control.' Jim Kelly could control a football game. Everyone knows we ran the no-huddle offense, and Jim Kelly had to call a play every 20 seconds. He didn't have the aid of a headset. He just went off what he felt would work at the time. He controlled the tempo of the game—fast, medium, ultrafast—run, pass, enough passing to keep the receivers happy, enough running to keep the linemen happy, and enough pace to wear the defense down. Nobody, *nobody* controlled a game better than Jim Kelly."

As Smith wiped away beads of perspiration and tears of joy at his own Canton induction speech, he expressed his gratitude for those who had taken part in his long road to success. He remembered how his high school football coach in Virginia, Cal

Davidson, had been instrumental in his career. "The temperature was in the mid-90s," Bruce said. "The humidity was high, and the training was rigorous. The first day was a nightmare. The second day, I quit. Cal called my house on that day and spoke with my father. After the conversation my father came and asked me, 'Son, why weren't you at practice today? Are you sick? Is something wrong?' I answered, 'No, sir, football is just too hard. It's too hot and it's too painful.' My father gave me a look that I never will forget. And in this baritone voice he said, 'Son, whatever you do in life, don't ever quit.'"

And the son never looked back or backed down, a quality that was no doubt integral in him earning the greatest honor his sport could bestow: his place in football's most exclusive fraternity. As he finished his speech, thanking so many teammates, he couldn't help but tweak his old running mate, Thomas: "My life would be a little less bright if I didn't have you to laugh and joke with. P. S. I hid your helmet."

When Levy was chosen to present Thomas at the 2007 induction ceremonies, the veteran coach praised "Thurman's prodigious exploits. Look it up, Thurman: prodigious." The joke was greeted by laughter from the audience.

When it came time for Thurman to speak, he said, "Marv, contrary to the misconceptions that you may have regarding my expansive vocabulary, or lack thereof, I believe all these years you have maybe confused me with someone else, and that person would be Bruce." There was more laughter before Thurman said, "Sorry, Bruce. I really didn't mean to throw you under the bus."

"Marv, you are my inspiration," he continued. "I wanted to play my best because I never wanted to disappoint you. You made me feel like every extra effort I made for the Bills was appreciated."

And then he remembered what may have very well been the turning point in his career. A football lifer, a great player named Elijah Pitts who went on to become an assistant coach with the Bills, scouted young Thurman. "Elijah Pitts, you are definitely here with me today," Thomas said. "You've always been there with me since 1988, the day you walked into that gym in Stillwater, Oklahoma, and said, 'Thurman Thomas?' You heard dead silence. 'I'm Elijah Pitts from the Buffalo Bills. I played with the Green Bay Packers and Vince Lombardi.' Quickly I raised my hand. I said, 'Here I am, coach, right here.'" And from that day on, he was on the road to the NFL and the Super Bowl.

"In closing," Thomas told the fans in Canton, "to the fans of Buffalo. Every guy has probably stood up here in all of these Hall of Fame jackets and said they probably have the best fans in the world supporting them. I'm here to say that's hogwash. No fans are like my fans, like Bills fans. You were all out there freezing, spending hard-earned money to cheer us on. You guys are the best. I don't know how to thank you for the support our team has been shown over the years. It was a ride that none of us will ever forget. A ride we would all probably love to hop back on. Unfortunately we can't buy tickets for that ride anymore. But we will always have those memories."

The great Bills era came to be defined by the arc of one boot of the football, a kick that sailed just off course and changed the trajectory of a proud franchise. The Bills never came any closer to winning a Super Bowl than they did in Tampa. Today, as they look back on that game—forever haunted—they are left to wonder if the kick had been true, if they had indeed become champions that first time, would that have altered their history?

It is a difficult question to consider, but the men who played through those championship seasons have managed not only to move on with their lives but also to flourish, enriched by those proud years spent playing the game. Perhaps no one exemplifies that more so than Scott Norwood, who returned to Ralph Wilson Stadium for the first time since he retired and 20 years after that fateful night in Tampa to receive the Ralph C. Wilson Jr. Distinguished Service Award in 2011 for his contributions to the team and community. Norwood was being saluted for his involvement with the Camp Good Days and Special Times, enriching the lives of children battling cancer. As a community volunteer, he also reportedly donated $300 to the camp for every kick he made during his career.

A modest man, Norwood was deeply moved by the tribute. "It takes on a sense of how you handle yourself as a team member within the community," he said on that occasion. "And the service I provide, I guess you do that as an athlete and you realize you are a role model, that through your job you are representing the team, the organization, and yourself as well. My work with the camp and some of the other things were a little ancillary for a football player but are an important part of the position."

Norwood played with the Bills from 1985 until 1991, and now on this Sunday afternoon in November 2011, the fans in the sold-out stadium gave him a standing ovation. Perhaps in some other places, the reception would have been nowhere near as warm. "It feels terrific to be back," Norwood said. "Not so much in front of the camera and speaking with people in the media, but it's been nice to see some old teammates and old friends who I haven't seen in many years. The connections are long and deep here, and it's just a tremendous feeling to be back amongst everybody."

"I think coming back into this setting is definitely a time to look back," Norwood continued. "It's not something many of us do in our normal lives. It is a time of reflection. For what I had to give, I think I performed and maybe exceeded what I could do. I took it seriously while I was here and did the best I could in all situations. I handled myself the best I could."

It had been a long and winding road that brought Norwood and the rest of his teammates together. And it was a journey that began with Kelly and the rest of the wonderful players Polian and Levy assembled around him.

When Kelly had his day in the sun at Canton, Marv Levy introduced him, asking, "Is there anyone here from Buffalo today? Is there anyone back in Buffalo today?" There were more than 17,000 fans for the ceremony on August 3, 2002, and approximately three-quarters of them had made the drive from Buffalo, far outdistancing the contingent from Pittsburgh on hand to cheer the great Steelers wide receiver John Stallworth.

When it came time for Kelly to address the crowd, he began to choke up. He was taken by the moment and he knew what was to come. For his would be no ordinary valedictory address. Kelly went deep that afternoon, deeper than he had ever gone on any stage or any field. Toward the end of his 17-minute speech, he saluted his five-year-old son, Hunter, who was born with a fatal neurological disease.

"Hunter was born on Valentine's Day, my birthday, the son I always I've always wanted. I've dreamt what every father dreams about—playing catch in the backyard, going fishing, camping, everything that fathers and sons do. But within four months, my son was diagnosed with a fatal disease called Krabbe's leukodystrophy. The doctors told us to take him home and make him feel comfortable. And from that day, my wife and I decided to fight this disease. And so we made it our lifelong commitment to make sure that kids all over the world don't suffer like my son does. "Since the day I was selected, I prayed to God that my son would be here with me today. God has granted me that blessing. It's been written throughout my career that toughness is my trademark. Well, the toughest person I've ever met in my life is my hero, my soldier, my son, Hunter. I love you, buddy." It was a moving speech and a rare moment of private reflection from the quarterback.

That evening after Kelly's induction, the Bills held a large party in his honor at the Crowne Plaza Quaker Square hotel in Akron, a twenty minute ride up the road from Canton. A couple of thousand people had crowded into the main ball room, and upstairs the Bills were hosting a private affair for their entourage in a smaller meeting room. Levy, who had been inducted the previous summer and had introduced his quarterback at the ceremony that afternoon, was joined by some of the old Bills, including Thomas, as well as Jim's family and friends. And the man, Polian, who regarded Kelly as something of a son, was also there on the quarterback's night to remember.

"We're all talking and telling war stories, having fun," Polian recalled. "Marv had gone in [to the Hall], so that's the first reunion. And now Jim has gone in, so that's the second reunion. And we're all together and having a great time, and I looked up, and there was a window that looked out on the main ballroom where there were thousands of people dancing and there's all kinds of people taking pictures. And somebody came and said, you all need to go out and stand on the bandstand so people can cheer and. Jim could make his talk. So we all went out, and flashbulbs are popping, and people are cheering, it was just an incredible scene, almost like, well *exactly* like the welcome home after the first Super Bowl.

"And so the evening's wearing down," Polian continues, "and we're getting ready to leave, and I come across a couple that comes up to us on the street. He says to my wife and I: 'Would you mind signing an autograph and taking a picture?' I said, 'No, not at all. I'd be honored to do so.' So I did. Then I said, 'Let me ask you something. This is Jim's night. What do you want my autograph for? You know, Jim's the guy who did this all, and it's great to be a part of it, but it's his night.' And the man turned to me and he said, 'You know, it's our way to say...'" And even now, years later, Polian's voice begins to strain. "I almost can't get this out," he apologizes. "'It's our way of saying thank you to you. You gave us the greatest times of our lives.'"

Bill Polian could barely finish this story he so much wanted to tell as he began to cry. "To me," he was finally able to say, "that captures what that relationship was and remains my experience to this day. I'm so privileged and honored to be part of it. What a privilege to have that experience, to be with those guys."

Acknowledgments

J OE CIFFA, WHO works with the Bills alumni and helped track down so many of the Super Bowl Bills and their loyal fans. The Bills public relations directors then and now, Denny Lynch and Scott Berchtold, for their assistance with research and recollections. Joe Horrigan and Pete Fierle of the Pro Football Hall of Fame for their research assistance. Tricia Cavalier and Emily Pricola of the Kelly for Kids Foundation who confirmed several details in this book. Vic Carucci and Sal Paolantonio, who helped me reach many of the former players and coaches who make up the heart of this era.

My friends, Sal Marchiano and Jeremy Schaap, who read the first draft of the opening chapter and urged me to pursue this story.

Janet Parson, more than my agent, for her guidance and support across the last three decades.

David Black, my esteemed literary agent, who was eager to take on this project and offered encouragement, guidance, and saw this to fruition.

And, always, my family. This story came about one wintry morning when the five of us were making breakfast in our sunlit kitchen, as we often do on those increasingly rare days when we're all together. It was then that I first broached the idea of trying to write a book—perhaps one about sports and perseverance and comebacks. The stuff of legends. And this is what I came upon. The Bills are the first team our son rooted for and the one we followed out to Pasadena, celebrating his eighth birthday at the Super Bowl. That game didn't turn out the way we hoped it would, but, hopefully, this book has been able to put all the wins and losses in perspective. All the good times sports can give us. Those moments of great expectations and endless joy. Memories that fill our lifetimes. Those Bills sure did that.

Sources

Books

Carucci, Vic. *The Buffalo Bills and the Almost-Dream Season*. New York: Simon & Schuster, 1991.

Gehman, Jim. *"Then Levy Said to Kelly…"* Chicago: Triumph Books. 2008.

Kelly, Jim with Vic Carucci. *Armed and Dangerous*. New York: Doubleday, 1992.

Levy, Marv with Jeff Miller. *Game Changers: The Greatest Plays in Buffalo Bills Football History*. Chicago: Triumph Books, 2009.

Periodicals

Bob Baptist, "Bills' Defense Clamps Down On Broncos." *The Columbus Dispatch*, January 13, 1992.

"Bills Will 'Hoop' It Up at Canisius in Benefit for Youths," *The Buffalo News*, April 7, 1993.

John F. Bonfatti, "Bills Hand Raiders Their Fist Loss." Associated Press, October 7, 1990.

Vic Carucci, "Kelly Says Hit Ballard's Fault Non-Block Led to Injury." *The Buffalo News*, October 10, 1989.

Greg Cote, "Thurman Thomas Something Left to Prove." *Miami Herald*, January 24, 1992.

Donna Ditota, "Bills Can't Believe They Won." *The (Syracuse) Post-Standard*, September 30, 1990.

Mike Freeman, "Premature Kicks, Missing Helmets—Murphy's Law Befalls Bills." *The Washington Post,* January 27, 1992.

Greg Garber, "Norwood Returns to Site of Super Miss." ESPN.com, January 30, 2001.

Thomas George, "It's Fourth-and-Heartbreak As the Bills Lose One More." *The New York Times,* January 30, 1994.

Thomas George, "The Redskins, and the Roof, Fall on the Bills." *The New York Times,* January 27, 1992.

Thomas George, "Super Bowl XXV: The Kickers; Unexpected Tight Finish," *The New York Times,* January 27, 1991.

Karl Taro Greenfield, "A Life After Wide Right." *Sports Illustrated,* July 12, 2004.

Craig Harvey, "Norwood Back in Buffalo to Receive Distinguished Service Award." *The Observer,* November 7, 2011.

Al Harvin, "Bills Are Bickering in Mid-Season Form." *The New York Times,* September 20, 1990.

John Hawkins, "Bennett Occupies Redskins' Minds." *The Washington Times,* January 13, 1992.

"Interview With Diana Dillaway" BuffaloRising.com, June 14, 2006.

Richard Justice, "Redskins Steal the Show: Washington Controls Bills in Super Bowl." *The Washington Post,* January 27, 1992.

Peter King, "Monday Morning Quarterback." SI.com, October 25, 2011.

Brandon Koch. "Norwood Honored with Distinguished Service Award." *Niagara (New York) Gazette,* November 7, 2011.

Leigh Montville, "Wide to The Right, Forever," *Sports Illustrated,* February 18, 1991.

Milt Northrop, "Kelly Apologizes for Blasting Ballard." *The Buffalo News,* October 13, 1989.

Mike Penner, "Bills' Kelly Filling the Airwaves." *Los Angeles Times,* January 22, 1992.

Don Pierson, "Bills Leave No Doubt, Rout Chiefs." *Chicago Tribune,* January 6, 1992.

Terry Price, "Bills Wouldn't Miss It for the World; A Can't Miss Oportunity," *The Hartford Courant.* January 14, 1992.

Dave Seminara, "The Greatest Rally or the Biggest Fade." *The New York Times,* January 2,

Gary Shelton, "Norwood Can't Miss In Buffalo." *Chicago Tribune,* September 29, 1991.

Gary Shelton, "Triple-Threat Thomas Runs, Receives, Whines." *St. Petersburg (Florida) Times,* January 24, 1992.

Jay Skurski, "A Humbled Hansen Shares Big Day with Family, Friends." *The Buffalo News,* September 18, 2011

Timothy W. Smith, "Cowboys Win 52–17." *The New York Times,* January 31, 1993.

Timothy W. Smith, "Cowboys Win 30–13." *The New York Times,* January 30, 1994.

Timothy W. Smith, "For Bills, a Bitter Taste of Defeat." *The New York Times,* January 27, 1992.

"Smith's Knee Causing Buffalo More Concern." *Toronto Star,* January 8, 1992.

Jerry Sullivan, "Boys to Men: Super Bowl Bills Realize They Had the Time of Their Lives." *The Buffalo News,* January 31, 2011.

Jerry Sullivan, "Tasker Elevates Bills' Depth Chart to New Heights." *The Buffalo News.* May 8, 1996.

Gene Wojciechowski, "He's Making Beeline to Recognition," *Los Angeles Times,* October 15, 1989.

Paul Zimmerman, "Big D, As In Dynasty." *Sports Illustrated,* February 8, 1993.

Videos

America's Game, "1990 Buffalo Bills," Produced by NFL Network.

America's Game, "The Super Bowl Champions, 1992 Cowboys," Produced by NFL Network.

Meet the Press. Tim Russert, host. Produced by NBC News, January 31, 1993.

"Scott Norwood Receives Distinguished Service Award." Bryan Shaw, WIVB-TV. November 7, 2011.

Super Bowl XXV. Produced by ABC Sports. January 27, 1991

30 For 30: Elway To Marino. Produced by ESPN.

Websites

BuffaloBills.com

ESPN.com

NFL.com

SI.com

YouTube.com

Speeches

Jim Kelly Hall of Fame Enshrinement Speech. August 3, 2002. Pro Football Hall of Fame. Canton, Ohio.

James Lofton Hall of Fame Enshrinement Speech. August 3, 2003. Pro Football Hall of Fame. Canton, Ohio.

Thurman Thomas Hall of Fame Enshrinement Speech. August 5, 2007. Pro Football Hall of Fame. Canton, Ohio.

Bruce Smith Hall of Fame Enshrinement Speech. August 8, 2009. Pro Football Hall of Fame. Canton, Ohio.

Interviews

Donn Bartz	Jimmy Johnson	Don Pitts
Cornelius Bennett	Jim Kelly	Bill Polian
Don Beebe	Mark Kelso	Andre Reed
Vic Carucci	Bob Koshinski	Frank Reich
Angelo Coniglio	Marv Levy	Jim Ritcher
Bob Coniglio	Denny Lynch	Darryl Talley
Dennis DiPaolo	Pete Metzelaars	Steve Tasker
Larry Felser	Peter Nussbaum	Jeff Wright
Kent Hull	Bill Parcells	Richard Zolnowski